JOHN MILTON

KENNETH MUIR

JOHN MILTON

LONGMANS

LONGMANS, GREEN AND CO LTD
48 Grosvenor Street, London W.1

*Associated companies, branches and representatives
throughout the world*

First published 1955
New edition by photolithography 1960
Second impression 1962
Third impression 1965
Fourth impression 1968

PRINTED IN GREAT BRITAIN
BY JOHN DICKENS & CO LTD
NORTHAMPTON

To

BONAMY DOBRÉE

ACKNOWLEDGEMENTS

I have to thank Mr. John Lehmann for permission to use some paragraphs from an essay of mine which appeared in *Penguin New Writing* in 1945. I am also grateful to the following for permission to quote passages:

Mr. W. MacKellar and the Yale University Press, Mr. W. Skeat and the Oxford University Press, Miss Helen Waddell and *The Listener* (for versions of the Latin poems); Mr. J. B. Leishman and John Murray; Dr. E. M. W. and Mrs. P. B. Tillyard and the Cambridge University Press; Professor F. A. Patterson and the Columbia University Press.

I have used the following initials to denote the translations quoted.

(C) : Columbia
(F) : Fellowes (*The Second Defence*, Bohn ed.)
(H) : Hanford (see Bibliography, p. 191)
(M): MacKellar
(T) : Tillyard

PREFACE

IT is impossible to separate Milton's life and works: his prose cannot be understood without some knowledge of his life and times, and his life cannot be understood without a thorough knowledge of the autobiographical passages in his prose and verse. I have therefore discussed the content of his prose works in chapters dealing with his life, though I have added a short chapter on his prose style. In a book of this kind it was.neither possible nor expedient to discuss many of Milton's minor works, but the Bibliography will, I hope, do something to repair my omissions.

For various reasons, any book about Milton is liable to arouse undue irritation in some of its readers, and the controversies his work inspires are 'not without dust and heat'. Even in such a brief book it was impossible to ignore the controversies, but I have tried not to increase the heat.

Every writer on Milton must be deeply indebted to his predecessors, and I have learnt as much from those with whom I often disagree, such as Mr. Eliot and Dr. Leavis, as from those with whom I have generally agreed. I have learnt a great deal from Professor W. R. Parker, with whom I discussed Milton some twenty-five years ago, although I have recorded my disagreement with some of his theories. I have to acknowledge the helpful criticism of my colleagues, Mr. K. Allott, Mr. A. Davenport and Mr. E. Schanzer, who read the book in manuscript.

For the English poems I have relied mainly on the original texts; for the English prose works on the

Columbia edition, although I have occasionally emended the punctuation; for the Latin verse I have used four different translations, including my own; and for the Latin prose I have used eclectically the Bohn, Tillyard and Columbia versions.

KENNETH MUIR

Liverpool, 1954

NOTE TO SECOND EDITION

I have corrected one or two obvious slips and added some recent titles to the bibliography, but I have not attempted to make more substantial changes. I do not now think, for example, that Milton's poetic powers were declining when he wrote the last books of *Paradise Lost.*

One or two friendly reviewers of the first edition complained that I had devoted too much space to the refutation of views which were obviously wrong. But I believe that when the book was written, some six years ago, there was so much prejudice against Milton, and not merely in academic circles, that it would have been impossible to ignore it. Perhaps I made too many concessions to the opposition.

KENNETH MUIR

Liverpool, 1960.

CONTENTS

Chapter One

INTRODUCTION

'HE cuts us all out—and the Ancients too.' So Dryden exclaimed after reading *Paradise Lost*; and in a verse epigram he proclaimed with some extravagance that Milton combined the qualities of the two greatest poets of antiquity;

> The first in loftiness of thought surpass'd,
> The next in majesty, in both the last:
> The force of Nature could no farther go;
> To make a third, she join'd the former two.

Pope, the next great poet, said that Milton's style was exotic rather than natural; but he added that 'as his subject lies a good deal out of the world it has a particular propriety in these parts of the poem.' He pointed out in the Postscript to his translation of the *Odyssey* that Milton is sparing of his exotic words and phrases when he is narrating earthly matters; and in the Preface to the *Iliad* he declared that the rarest and most valuable quality of poetry is the '*vivida vis animi*':

> Where this appears, tho' attended with absurdities, it brightens all the Rubbish about it, 'till we see nothing but its own Splendor. . . . In *Milton*, it glows like a Furnace kept up to an uncommon Fierceness by the Force of Art: In *Shakespeare*, it strikes before we are aware, like an accidental Fire from Heaven.

Johnson disliked Milton's character and politics, and he

was prejudiced against blank verse. He declared, never-theless, that *Paradise Lost* was

> a poem, which, considered with respect to design, may claim the first place, and with respect to performance the second, among the productions of the human mind. . . . His work is not the greatest of heroick poems, only because it is not the first.

To the Romantic poets—Shelley and Keats, as well as Coleridge and Wordsworth—Milton was second only to Shakespeare; and though Keats, when he abandoned the second *Hyperion*, decided that *Paradise Lost*, 'though so fine, was a corruption of our language', he was swayed in his opinion by his failure to eliminate Miltonic inversions from his own poem, and by his wish to 'devote himself to other sensations.' Shelley spoke of the supremacy of Milton's genius. Wordsworth invoked Milton's soul to

> return to us again;
> And give us manners, virtue, freedom, power.

Landor thought *Paradise Lost* was 'the noblest specimen in the world of eloquence, harmony, and genius'. To Tennyson, Milton was the 'God-gifted organ-voice of England'. The best of the Victorian critics, Matthew Arnold, declared that Milton was

> by his diction and rhythm the one artist of the highest rank whom we have; this I take as requiring no discussion, this I take as certain. . . . Milton has made the great style no longer an exotic here; he has made it an inmate amongst us, a leaven, and a power.

Hopkins, who like Newman thought Milton 'a very bad man' because he consented 'to those who break the sacred bond of marriage', and Bridges, who regarded him as heroically virtuous, agreed on his greatness as poet. Indeed, if one had asked any competent critic between

1700 and 1900 about Milton's place, they would all have replied that, with the exception of Shakespeare, Milton was the greatest of English poets.

Now, in the last forty years, there has been a startling change. Ezra Pound and T. S. Eliot, realizing that the shadow of the Miltonic sublime prevented the development of modern poetry, began a campaign against it. 'It invariably happens', wrote Mr. Eliot in 1947, 'that the young poets engaged in such a revolution' in poetic diction will 'depreciate the merits of poets who do not stand for the qualities which they are zealous to realize.' Mr. Middleton Murry had other reasons for his criticisms of Milton. He argued in *Keats and Shakespeare* that Keats, after being under the Miltonic influence for about a year, while he was writing *Hyperion* and most of his other great poems, turned back to Chatterton and Shakespeare, wrote *To Autumn*, decided to come to terms with his public, instead of scorning it, and returned also to Fanny Brawne. Murry followed the Keats of the autumn of 1819 in branding the Miltonic style as foreign; and elsewhere he attacked Milton's egotism and sinful pride. It should be said, however, that nearly all Keats's greatest poetry was written while he was under the influence of Milton, and Mr. Eliot has pointed out that '*King Stephen* was more blighted by Shakespeare than *Hyperion* by Milton.' Just as 'Milton made a great epic impossible for succeeding generations,' so 'Shakespeare made a great poetic drama impossible.' Dr. F. R. Leavis in a brilliant and influential essay, published in *Scrutiny* and afterwards reprinted in *Revaluation*, could state with an air of finality:

> Milton's dislodgement in the past decade, after two centuries of predominance, was effected with remarkably little fuss. The irresistible argument was, of course, Mr. Eliot's creative achievement; it gave his few critical asides—potent,

it is true, by context—their finality, and made it unnecessary to elaborate a case. Mr. Middleton Murry, also, it should be remembered, came out against Milton at much the same time. His *Problem of Style* contains an acute page or two comparing Milton with Shakespeare. . . . Mr. Tate thinks that if we don't like Milton it is because of a prejudice against myth and fable. . . . Our objection to Milton, it must be insisted, is that we dislike his verse and believe that in such verse no 'highly sensuous and perfectly make-believe world' could be evoked.

In the rest of his essay Dr. Leavis tried to show by a detailed examination of certain passages of blank verse that the style of *Paradise Lost* and of the later poems shows a disastrous deterioration and ossification compared with that of *Comus*. He admitted in a later pronouncement that he regarded Milton as a great genius, but when Mr. Eliot modified his previous view, Dr. Leavis took him severely to task.

Mr. Eliot's earlier asides, which were supposed to have been so devastating in their effect, do not perhaps after this lapse of time appear either so witty or so potent as they once did. To describe Satan as 'a curly-haired Byronic hero', to say that Milton's 'celestial and infernal regions are large but insufficiently furnished apartments filled by heavy conversation', or to say that the Puritan mythology is 'thin' would pass as table-talk, but they would not have effected Milton's 'dislodgement' unless the general public had been glad of an excuse to lapse into a '*Nil admirari*' of a poet they admired rather than loved.

To many Mr. Eliot's confession of distaste for Milton's character came as a welcome relief after a century of idolatry:

As a man, he is antipathetic. Either from the moralist's point of view, or from the theologian's point of view, or

> from the psychologist's point of view, or judging by the ordinary standards of likeableness in human beings, Milton is unsatisfactory.

This schoolmasterly report was received with some satisfaction by the general reader because his reverence for Milton had for some time been traditional and conventional. Between the seventeenth century and the twentieth two things had been happening which had gradually reduced the enjoyment and even the understanding of Milton's poetry: the decline of religious faith and the abandonment of the 'grand old fortifying classical curriculum'. To Milton's contemporaries, whether Puritan or Royalist, *Paradise Lost* was an epic on the greatest of all subjects, and it expressed a theology to which everyone more or less subscribed. But few people now believe in the literal truth of the *Book of Genesis*, and those who do are not normally serious readers of poetry. At the same time the neglect of the classics has meant inevitably that Milton's later verse seems to be written in a dead language. Dryden, Johnson, Coleridge and Arnold had all studied Greek and Latin.

We can be debarred from appreciating Milton's work by religious conviction, and still more by lack of it. We can be separated from him politically if we regard the Good Old Cause as evil, and though Whigs and Radicals, Marxists and Social Democrats, have found plenty to admire in Milton's political pamphlets—and in so far as his poems contain similar views they have been willing to include them in their approbation—yet they have often misinterpreted the poet by regarding his religious views as comparatively unimportant, or by failing to recognize that neither his political nor his religious views were static. These views have thus been praised as democratic or condemned as authoritarian by those who

can read history only through twentieth-century spectacles.

Now the animosities aroused by Milton's character, his
politics, and his religion would not greatly matter if they
did not affect our judgement of his prose and poetry; and
as he himself always insisted that only a great and good
man could write great poetry it would be wrong to
attempt to separate the man from his work. But this
means that it is very difficult to enjoy his work, whether
in prose or verse, if we regard his convictions with
aversion, for those convictions inevitably intrude themselves. By a curious irony, during the years when Milton
was being dislodged he was by other critics being interpreted more adequately than ever before. The numerous studies of his prose, his poetry, his theology and his
politics have uncovered a new complexity and depth in
his work. He has been revealed as a great humanist as
well as the great Puritan, as the eloquent spokesman of
the changing phases of the English Revolution, and as a
brilliant and independent theologian who yet contrived
to write the great epic of orthodox Christianity. In a
sense, as Eliot has said, he is now 'folded into a single
party' with his political and religious opponents: both
sides differed from the majority of modern readers in
believing that religion was supremely important. It
seems to have been Eliot's realization of this fact which
led him to his later, and more generous, estimate of
Milton as a poet, especially as the poetic revolution led
by himself and Pound had been successful.

Yet Leavis is perfectly right to insist that from the
standpoint of the literary critic all such questions are
subordinate to that of poetic quality. It may have been
tactically expedient for Eliot to denigrate Milton, as it
had been expedient for Wordsworth and Keats to attack
Pope; but this tells us very little about the actual poetic

merits of Milton or Pope, except that their influence on their successors has been as unhappy as it was considerable. The question which we have to answer is not whether Milton's influence was a good one, nor whether we happen to agree with his views on divorce, King Charles, Original Sin, and the Trinity, nor even whether Satan or Adam is the real hero of *Paradise Lost*, nor whether Milton was a humanist or a Puritan, but whether in fact Milton deteriorated as a poet after 1638.

It is possible to argue with Keats that a poet should make 'his mind a thoroughfare for all thoughts and not a select party', and that Milton by falling into the habit of political controversy lost the sensitiveness he had once possessed. Twenty years of prose, both Latin and English, and a diet of books unappetising in themselves and unlikely to increase his store of images, may have seriously impoverished his imagination and driven him to adopt an artificial style which would cloak his poverty. Wordsworth continued to write long after his sensibility had become permanently impoverished, but all his best poetry was based on memories of childhood and youth, while Milton's very different education deprived him of the thing Wordsworth possessed in such abundance. Childhood to Milton recalled mainly the school bench, the city streets, the smell of midnight oil—and headaches. As a preparation for his poetic vocation it was not ideal: it was saved only by music—and, of course, the reading of poetry. It was doubtless the weakness of Milton's eyes and his eventual blindness that led him to make use of what Dryden calls the spectacles of books to assist the deficiencies of his visual imagination.

Yet in spite of the limitations of his endowments and of the nature of his education, Milton—to use his favourite text—was made perfect in weakness. In his five major poems he was led by an unerring instinct to choose

B

themes where his poetic virtues could be most manifest, and his weaknesses, and the weaknesses of the Puritan way of life, least damaging. Even the postponement of his poem on the Fall, which some critics have lamented, enabled him to bring to the subject a much wider range of experience than it would otherwise have possessed; and if he bought the grand style at a heavy price, there is no reason to doubt that the price was worth paying.

Chapter Two

EDUCATION

ABOUT the time that Shakespeare turned from tragedy to romance, on 9 December 1608, John Milton was born in Bread Street, Cheapside, at the sign of the Spread Eagle. Here his father, after whom the poet was named, carried on the profession of scrivener. The elder Milton was a talented composer, who had been one of the contributors to *The Triumphs of Oriana*, a book of madrigals in honour of Queen Elizabeth. He came of an Oxfordshire family, neighbours of the Powells, and he had been disinherited by his Roman Catholic family when he turned Protestant. He had made a sacrifice for his beliefs, even though he became wealthy by means of his profession and financial speculation. He married Sarah Jeffrey, a tailor's daughter, about whom little is known except that she was virtuous and charitable, and that she had weak eyesight. Three children of the marriage survived infancy. An elder sister, Anne, married when the poet was fourteen, and became the mother of Edward and John Phillips, the poet's pupils and biographers. A younger brother, Christopher, born in 1615, became a Royalist, a Catholic, and a lawyer, ending up as one of James II's judges. Milton was to have harsh things to say of Royalists, Catholics and lawyers, but he seems to have remained to the end of his life on good terms with his brother.

Milton was sent to the neighbouring school of St. Paul's, probably at the age of seven. He was taught by the

headmaster's son, Alexander Gill, a man who was afterwards to drink a toast to the murderer of the Duke of
Buckingham. Milton kept up correspondence with him
after he left school. He was coached, either before or
during his schooldays, by Thomas Young, one of the five
authors of the Smectymnuus pamphlets. At school the
poet's closest friend was Charles Diodati, who was the
grandson of a Protestant exile from Italy, and who became
a doctor and died while Milton was in Italy.

It was recognized early that Milton was a boy of ex-
ceptional promise, and his father took great pains to
ensure that the promise was not wasted through lack of
training. The maid was instructed to sit up with the boy
as he literally burned the midnight oil, and the failure of
his eyesight may be traced, at least in part, to the strain it
endured in childhood. Milton himself tells us:

> My father destined me while yet a boy for the study of
> humane letters, which I seized with such eagerness that from
> the twelfth year of my age I scarcely ever went from my
> lessons to bed before midnight; which, indeed, was the first
> cause of injury to my eyes, to whose natural weakness there
> were also added frequent headaches. (H)

It has recently been argued by Professor Hanford that
Milton was a backward child, and that he suffered all his life
from the traumatic effects of his backwardness. It is true
that he went up to Cambridge when he was sixteen years
of age, and this is rather later than the average; but it is
probable that he was unspecialized rather than backward. He had studied subjects outside the normal curriculum—French, Italian, and Music—as well as the usual
Latin, Greek, Rhetoric and a little Hebrew. He was
doubtless kept back by his frequent headaches; but his
later relations with Gill and Young suggest that he was a
brilliant and favourite pupil. He was already beginning

to write verse, as Aubrey tells us, and the metrical versions of the psalms done at the age of fifteen were carefully preserved for publication over twenty years later.

He matriculated in April 1625, and he went up to Christ's College, Cambridge, soon after the accession of Charles I. He quarrelled with his tutor, William Chappell, and he was rusticated for a time. Perhaps, as Aubrey reports, he was whipped. In the first of the Latin elegies, written to Charles Diodati, Milton told his friend that he was not anxious to return to Cambridge as it was not a suitable place for writing verse. 'Nor does it suit me always to endure the threats of a harsh master, and other wrongs to which my nature will not submit.' He seems to have enjoyed his temporary exile, reading, writing, and going to the theatre; and the poem ends with a eulogy of London maidens whom Milton had admired from a discreet distance. The reason why he was rusticated is not known. As Chappell was opposed to the reform of the curriculum, and as Milton in his *Prolusions* comes out in favour of the reformers, they may have quarrelled on this subject. History, mathematics and science were excluded from the curriculum. Dorislaus, the first Baconian lecturer, gave offence by seeming to speak 'too much in defence of the liberties of the people', and the lectureship was therefore suspended. Milton had read Bacon's works before he went up to Cambridge, and his sympathies were entirely with the progressive party. Speeches on traditional topics, delivered in Latin, were the only means of obtaining a degree, and we find Milton in the third prolusion attacking the very system in which he was participating. He felt that such training was a useless preparation for life. It made the graduate 'a more finished fool and a cleverer contriver of conceits', but quite incapable of coping with the problems he would meet in the real world. Elsewhere Milton frankly confesses his boredom with his own speech. It was not to be expected that such outspokenness would be well-received, though the poet seems to have had no trouble with his second tutor, Nathaniel Tovey. If by the end of his stay at Cambridge Milton had earned the respect of the dons, as undoubtedly he did, it was partly due to his manifest ability in performing the academic exercises he despised. By luck or by design he was given subjects in which he could express his own convictions, and if necessary he could twist the subject for his own purposes. His attack on the scholastic philosophy (*Prol.* 3) and the defence of learning (*Prol.* 7) were opportunities of which he made the most; but he also contrived to insert a favourite idea about the music of the spheres (*Prol.* 2) and an eloquent passage about the Roman Empire (*Prol.* 5), in order to show that he stood with the reformers in wishing to introduce the study of history into the curriculum.

At first, it appears, Milton was unpopular with his fellow-undergraduates. He was, perhaps, intellectually arrogant; and his purity of life and something effeminate in his appearance earned him the nickname of the Lady of Christ's. Yet, as he was careful to point out, he was athletic, ruddy complexioned, and skilful with his sword. By the end of his third year he seems to have triumphed over these initial difficulties with dons and students, and in his sixth prolusion he thanked his former opponents for their change of attitude towards him.

> I am quite overcome with pride and joy at finding myself surrounded on all sides by such an assembly of learned men; and yet, when I take stock of myself and turning my eyes inward contemplate in my own heart the meagre powers I possess, I blush to myself and a sudden uprush of modesty overwhelms and chokes my rising joy. (T)

The speech which follows is full of puns and somewhat

Rabelaisian humour. Milton felt he could afford to relax; and in the last part of this prolusion he abandoned the customary Latin, 'leaping over the academic rules', and introduced the verses, afterwards entitled 'At a Vacation Exercise', in which he gave public expression to his poetic ambitions and dismissed the fashionable poetry of the day as

> those new fangled toys, and triming slight
> Which takes our late fantasticks with delight.

The poem is interesting as it apparently marks Milton's determination to write poetry in his native language, although nearly all his verse up till now had been written in Latin; the 'Elegy on a Fair Infant', written in memory of his niece, the 'fairest flower no sooner blown but blasted', is the only English poem, except the paraphrases of the psalms, Milton had so far composed. But he had in his first years at Cambridge already written seven or eight Latin poems. They included the elegy addressed to Diodati, from which we have quoted, elegies on a university beadle, on Bishop Lancelot Andrewes, on the Bishop of Ely, and on the Vice-Chancellor, a poem addressed to Young, by then a chaplain in Hamburg, and a poem which seems to record an early experience of love, which some have linked with the Italian sonnets to 'Emilia', and with the English sonnet addressed to the nightingale, though these were probably written a year or two later. Most of the Latin poems are mere poetic exercises, but we need not suppose that Milton was being insincere in speaking of Andrewes as a soul half-divine. More interesting is the miniature epic on the Gunpowder Plot, the anniversary of which was celebrated by thanksgiving services and commemorative verses. Warton suggested that 'this little Poem, as containing a council, conspiracy, and expedition of Satan, may be considered as an early and promising prolusion of Milton's genius to the *Paradise Lost*.' The poem, in spite of the violent attack on the Pope to be expected of a young Puritan, is sufficiently powerful to have tempted him to go on writing in Latin.

That Milton had other ambitions as well as poetic ones can be seen from the last of the prolusions in which he declares that he has taken all knowledge for his province and in which he describes the honours with which the great scholar is rewarded :.

> To be the oracle of many nations, to find one's home re-garded as a kind of temple, to be a man whom kings and states invite to come to them, whom men from near and far flock to visit, while to others it is a matter of pride if they have but set eyes on him once. These are the rewards of study, these are the prizes which learning can and often does bestow upon her votaries in private life. (T)

These words were written in 1631 or 1632 and by this time Milton had already composed his first poetic master-pieces. These included the Latin poem 'On the Approach of Spring' and the Nativity Ode, both written in 1629, the song 'On May Morning' and the lines on Shakespeare (1630), the 'Epitaph on the Marchioness of Winchester', 'L'Allegro' and 'Il Penseroso'. In a Latin poem addressed to Diodati, in which Milton mentions the writing of the Nativity Ode, he describes the life of austerity proper to the epic poet:

> He indeed must live sparely, after the manner of Pythagoras, and herbs must supply his harmless fare. Let only the crystal-clear water in a beechen bowl stand near him, and let him drink temperate draughts from the pure spring. More than this, his youth must be chaste and free from sin, his manner strict, and his hand without stain. . . . After this manner, they say, wise Tiresias lived when the light of his eyes was

gone. . . . Truly the bard is sacred to the gods; he is their priest, and both his heart and lips mysteriously breathe the indwelling Jove. (M)

Milton, therefore, wished to be a great scholar and an epic poet, and he had at one time intended to enter the ministry and perhaps become a don at Cambridge. But his dislike of the Cambridge curriculum and his increasing dislike of episcopacy ruled out both possibilities. Ten years later he told his readers that he had been destined from childhood for the Church.

> till coming to some maturity of years and perceiving what tyranny had invaded the Church, that he who would take orders must subscribe slave, and take an oath withal, which unless he took with a conscience that would retch, he must either straight perjure or split his faith, I thought it better to prefer a blameless silence before the sacred office of speaking bought, and begun with servitude and forswearing.

Soon after leaving Cambridge (or, as some think, in 1637) he addressed his father in Latin verse, excusing himself for his long preparation for his life's work, and urging his father to be patient with him until his education as a poet was complete.

According to Milton's own account he spent five years, from 1632 to 1638, at his father's estate, and until recently it was assumed that this was at Horton in Buckinghamshire; but it now seems that most of this period was spent at Hammersmith[1] where his father had recently acquired a house; they probably lived there until the spring of 1635, when they moved to Horton; Hammersmith was then in the country and Milton had the advantages of healthy surroundings and comparative solitude, while proximity to London enabled him to visit

[1] Cf. Harris Fletcher, *Journal of English and Germanic Philology* (1952), pp. 154-9.

the bookshops and take lessons in music and mathematics. During these five years Milton set himself an enormous programme of reading, and the seriousness with which he applied himself to his task may be gauged from his Commonplace Book, into which he copied extracts and summaries from his reading on a variety of topics. According to Professor Hanford, Milton began, apparently

> with the records of early Christianity in Eusebius and his continuers, turning aside to study the writing of the Fathers themselves: Clement, Cyprian, Ignatius, Tertullian, Justin Martyr. The contemporary secular history of the Greek Empire was represented by Procopius and the later Byzantines, that of Rome by Sigonius and others.

Later on he was

> long occupied with the obscure history of Italy under the Lombards, Franks, and Germans to the moment when that nation was emancipated by Rudolph, king of Germany.

He then proceeded to study the history of Venice and other city-states. But history is only one of his many branches of study, and he must have got through the preliminary reading for *Christian Doctrine* and his unfinished *Thesaurus*. He read not for the sake of acquiring considerable learning, but as a preparation for his life's work; and there is evidence that he was already interested in divorce, the government of the Church, and politics in general.

It is interesting to find, for example, a large number of passages relating to monarchy. Milton quotes Severus Sulpicius to the effect that 'the name of king has always been hateful to free peoples' and from Machiavelli the view that 'a commonwealth is to be preferred to a monarchy'. On the discommodities of marriage, Milton refers to the Wife of Bath's Prologue in *The Canterbury*

Tales. He quotes views that divorce may be permitted for desertion, or for difference of religion. He refers to Lactantius's opinion that evil is necessary for the attesting and training of virtue, but he reproves Lactantius and Tertullian for their condemnation of plays.

> He does not even once seem to have reflected that, while the corrupting influences of the theatre ought to be eliminated, it does not follow that it is necessary to abolish altogether the performance of plays. This on the contrary would be quite senseless; for what in the whole of philosophy is more impressive, purer, or more uplifting than a noble tragedy, what more helpful to a survey at a single glance of the changes and chances of this mortal life?

Such a passage illustrates Milton's independence both from early authorities and from his fellow-puritans.

Milton's sense of responsibility in his studies is apparent in the letter to an unknown friend, of which there are two drafts in the Trinity College manuscript. This letter is interesting for a number of reasons. It is a considered statement, as the two drafts testify, of Milton's consciousness of being a dedicated spirit, and this consciousness runs through all his correspondence and his English and Latin verse. Again and again he alludes to the parable of the Talents, and it is the deep significance this parable has for him which imbues with such power his sonnet on his blindness. It is apparent from the letter that he had considered the possibility of marriage and had decided not to seek a wife until his education was complete. His ambitious programme of reading required solitude. It is apparent, too, that he regarded himself as committed to the Puritan side in the struggle which had already begun, and that he already regarded the other side as the enemy. Above all it is clear that he scorned the acquisition of knowledge for its own sake. This was

an unprofitable sin which turned a man into a useless
creature. The real purpose of knowledge was for use,
either in political and religious controversy, or as material
which the poet could use in his imaginative work.

Milton's friend had evidently been remonstrating with
him for his selfishness in burying himself in the country
for the purpose of continuing his studies, when he ought
to have been ordained so that he could preach the gospel,
or at least to have engaged actively in the struggle for
political and religious liberty. Milton's reply is evasive
and ambiguous. He leads his mentor to suppose that he
still intends to become a clergyman—by his reference to
preaching—but without committing himself in any way.
It is very unlikely that he still contemplated ordination,
and his real ambitions, about which he is deliberately
ambiguous, were almost certainly poetical ones. In the
course of the letter Milton quotes a sonnet, written some
time before; and though this was clearly a dedication to
poetry, it could be taken by his reader to refer to a more
directly religious service:

> How soon hath Time, the subtle thief of youth,
>   Stol'n on his wing my three-and-twentieth year!
>   My hasting days fly on with full career,
>   But my late spring no bud or blossom shew'th.
> Perhaps my semblance might deceive the truth
>   That I to manhood am arrived so near,
>   And inward ripeness doth much less appear,
>   That some more timely-happy spirits indu'th.
> Yet be it less or more, or soon or slow,
>   It shall be still in strictest measure even
>   To that same lot however mean or high
> Toward which Time leads me, and the will of Heaven:
>   All is, if I have grace to use it so,
>   As ever in my great Taskmaster's eye.

It has been suggested that the reference in the fourth line

to 'bud or blossom' was an allusion to the precocious Cowley's *Poetical Blossoms*, actually published in 1633, though Milton may have got wind of it some months before.

The first-fruits of Milton's new dedication were a group of religious poems—'On Time', 'Upon the Circumcision' and 'At a solemn Musick'. He may have intended to write more of such lyrics, but the success of his commissioned entertainment, 'Arcades', led to an invitation to write what proved to be the first of his major works, *Comus*. The other great poem of these years was also commissioned, though he may have begun to write 'Lycidas' before he received an invitation to contribute to the volume in memory of Edward King, a fellow of his old college. There are drafts of all these poems in the Trinity College Manuscript, and they provide precious evidence of the poet's methods of composition.

Two letters written by Milton to Diodati in the autumn of 1637, a few months after the death of the poet's mother, are interesting for the light they throw on the warmth of his feelings for the friend he was so soon to lose. Only to his father and Diodati did he reveal the full extent of his ambitions, and the Latin poem to his father may have been written now and not earlier:

It is impossible for me not to love men like you. God . . . has instilled into me, if into anyone, a vehement love of the beautiful. . . . It is my habit day and night to seek for this Idea of the beautiful, as for a certain image of supreme beauty, through all the forms and faces of things (for many are the shapes of things divine) and to follow it as it leads me on by some sure traces which I seem to recognize. Hence it is that, when anyone scorns what the vulgar opine in their depraved estimation of things, and dares to feel and speak and be that which the highest wisdom throughout all ages has taught to be best, to that man I attach myself forthwith by a kind of real necessity, wherever I find him. . . .

But now I know you wish to have your curiosity satisfied. You make many anxious inquiries, even as to what I am at present thinking of. . . . You ask what I am thinking of? So may the good Deity help me, of immortality! And what am I doing? Growing my wings and meditating flight; but as yet our Pegasus raises himself on very tender pinions. (C)

Milton goes on to describe his practical plans: to take chambers in one of the Inns of Court where he will have more comfort and more intellectual companionship than at Horton, and where he will be closer to the London bookshops. Before attempting to carry this plan into effect and before starting his epic poem, Milton decided to complete his education by a continental tour; and that tour, and the fruitful contacts it gave him with Italian poets and scholars, opens a new chapter in his life.

Chapter Three

EARLY POEMS

B Y the time Milton went on his continental tour he had written, with the exception of three sonnets and four Latin poems, all the contents of the 1645 volume, and this is a convenient place to assess the value of his early work. Although he had read and assimilated most of his predecessors in four or five languages, he acquired very early a style of his own. He told Dryden that Spenser had been his model, though few passages in his poems strike the reader as directly Spenserian. He was referring, no doubt, to the didactic element in the 'sage and serious Spenser' whom he pronounced to be a better teacher than Aquinas. There are traces, as we shall see, of Spenserian allegory in *Comus* and of Neoplatonism partly derived from Spenser in several of the poems; and in the juvenile poem on his infant niece he appears to be echoing Spenser's characteristic cadences. But super-ficially, at least, the influence of the minor Spenserians is more apparent than that of Spenser himself. His copy of William Browne is copiously annotated, and there are numerous echoes in his work of the poems of Giles and Phineas Fletcher; but Milton transformed the diluted charm of his models by greater concentration and by his unerring choice of diction, in much the same way as Keats converted lines from Mary Tighe into some of the finest passages in his Odes. Browne's influence is most apparent in the 'Epitaph on the Marchioness of Win-chester', but even in this early poem Milton far surpassed his model. Appropriately formal, it yet conveys in its grave octosyllabics the pathos of early death, and it softens the sadness by the prospect of immortality, by the introduction of poetic wit, and by the subtle music of the verse:

> Here be tears of perfect moan
> Wept for thee in *Helicon*,
> And som Flowers, and som Bays,
> For thy Hearse to strew the ways,
> Sent thee from the banks of *Came*. . . .

In this passage, referring apparently to poems written by other Cambridge poets, a delightful effect is obtained by the irregularity of the third line; and another passage, afterwards echoed by Andrew Marvell, exhibits equally Milton's early mastery of the octosyllabic couplet:

> But the fair blossom hangs the head
> Sideways, as on a dying bed,
> And those Pearls of dew she wears
> Prove to be presaging tears,
> Which the sad morn has let fall
> On her hast'ning funeral.

It is significant that Milton's first published poem was the tribute to Shakespeare in the Second Folio of his plays. The lines prove that he honoured Shakespeare's memory 'on this side idolatry as much as any', and they indicate perhaps why it was impossible to imitate his work. A poet in the seventeenth century was compelled to explore new poetic territories:

> What needs my *Shakespear* for his honour'd Bones,
> The labour of an age in piled Stones,
> Or that his hallow'd reliques should be hid
> Under a Star-ypointing *Pyramid*?
> Dear son of memory, great heir of Fame,
> What need'st thou such weak witnes of thy name?
> Thou in our wonder and astonishment
> Hast built thy self a live-long Monument.

Neither the conventional and misleading tribute in
'L'Allegro' to Fancy's child, warbling 'his native wood-
notes wilde', nor Milton's discreditable sneer at Charles
I for reading Shakespeare's plays in prison, nor even the
tart dismissal of Shakespeare and his fellows in the preface to *Samson Agonistes*, where he speaks of the Athenian
dramatists as 'unequall'd yet by any', can affect the mag-
nificence of his early tribute to '*my* Shakespeare'.

The poem ends with an ingenious conceit:

> Then thou, our fancy of it self bereaving,
> Dost make us Marble with too much conceiving;
> And, so Sepulcher'd, in such pomp dost lie,
> That Kings, for such a Tomb, would wish to die.

Shakespeare's readers, turned to marble by their admiration, provide him with a monument. The conceit was
suggested by the opening lines of Jonson's elegy, and Dr.
Tillyard describes the whole poem as Milton's one 'successful venture in the more extravagant, and at that date,
more vital type, of seventeenth-century verse'. When he
was at Cambridge the fashionable poets were the Meta-
physicals, but he deliberately turned his back on 'those
new-fangled toys'. He would probably have disapproved
of the subject-matter of Donne's love poems. He might,
however, have been expected to admire the poems of
George Herbert, but though Mr. Eliot is unfair when he
declares that Milton triumphed with a dazzling disregard
of the soul, he certainly lacked the humility of sainthood,
and he rejected the soul-searching, the conceits, and the
prosaic diction of the Metaphysical school. Moreover the
poems of Donne and Herbert were not published until
1633, when Milton had chosen his own path. He did not
altogether disdain the conceit in his youth, but his conceits generally belong to the Italian tradition. The Hobson poems are an exception that proves the rule, for they

C

consist of a light-hearted string of ingenious quibbles designed to appeal to the Cambridge wits. When he included two Hobson poems in his 1645 collection Milton took the trouble to revise them thoroughly; and a third poem on the same subject and in the same style, which had appeared in an anthology, was excluded from the collection because, if Milton was indeed the author, he did not wish to overweight his book with trifles. If the poem was written by someone else it will serve to illustrate the fact that Milton was deliberately trying his hand at a popular *genre*.

> Here *Hobson* lyes amongst his many debters,
> A man unlearned, yet of many letters:
> The Schollers well can testifie as much,
> That have receiv'd them from his pregnant pouch.
> His carriage was well knowne oft t'have begun,
> In Embassie 'twixt father and the Sonne.
> In *Cambridge* few (in good time be it spoken)
> But well remembreth him by some good token.
> From thence to London rode he day by day,
> Till death benighted him, he lost his way.
> No wonder is it, that he thus is gone,
> Since most men knew he long was drawing on.
> His Teame was of the best, nor could he have
> Bin mir'd in any ground, but in his grave:
> And there he stickes indeede, still at a stand,
> Vntill some Angell lende a helping hand.
> So rest in peace thou ever-toyling swaine,
> And supreame Waggoner, next to Charls-waine.

Milton's first masterpiece had been written two years before this, just after his twenty-first birthday. The 'Nativity Ode' is given pride of place in the 1645 volume, though Warton complained that it chiefly consisted 'of a string of affected conceits which his early youth, and the fashion of the times can only excuse'. A later critic, Elton, similarly declared that the poem 'is somewhat freely crossed with things that cannot be admired, with the overworked fancy and the unfortunate twist of imagery which are so fatal to masses of early Stuart verse'. The conceits, as Sir Herbert Grierson has pointed out, 'are not those of Donne and Cowley. They are those of Marino, Southwell and Crashaw.' One image has been universally condemned, though it has a charming absurdity which is not unattractive:

> So when the Sun in bed,
> Curtain'd with cloudy red,
>   Pillows his chin upon an Orient wave.

Milton outgrew his taste for baroque images, but the lack of complete sobriety in his early poems is a fault on the right side. Few readers to-day would approve of his later sacrifice of the charming line

> Th'enameld *Arras* of the Rain-bow wearing

which he altered in 1673 to the tame and decorous

> Orb'd in a Rain-bow; and like glories wearing
> Mercy will sit between . . .

The introductory stanzas are deliberately pitched in a low key. The Hymn itself is written in a difficult stanza, although Milton's skill in manipulating it makes it appear deceptively easy. Equally skilful are the way the stanza is varied to suit the content, the easy transitions from one stanza to the next, and the introduction, with perfect naturalness, of references to the Crucifixion and the Last Judgement. The description of winter in the first stanza leads naturally to Nature's prayer to cover her deformities with snow, with an implied contrast between Nature and Grace. Then Peace is sent as Christ's harbinger, and the next stanzas describe the temporary cessation of war and the supersession of the old order of kingship (as in Eliot's *Journey of the Magi*):

> And Kings sate still with awfull eye,
> As if they surely knew their sovran Lord was by.

The winds and waters are also pacified, and Milton goes
on to describe the homage paid by the stars and sun. The
reference to the sun leads to an account of the shepherds
watching their flocks before dawn, and at this point the
poem drops appropriately into the tone of the pastoral.
The song of the angels, heard by the shepherds, enables
Milton to introduce, from his own prolusion written just
before, a description of the music of the spheres, a theme
in which he could express his two chief passions—for
music and virtue.

> Ring out ye Chrystall spheares,
> Once bless our human ears,
>   (If ye have power to touch our senses so)
> And let your silver chime
> Move in melodious time;
>   And let the Base of Heav'ns deep Organ blow,
> And with your ninefold harmony
> Make up full consort to th'Angelike symphony.
>
> For if such holy Song
> Enwrap our fancy long,
>   Time will run back and fetch the age of gold . . .

From the Golden Age there is a natural transition to the redemption of Man and the Last Judgement, though since the
Nativity Satan's power has been limited. The old Dragon

> wrath to see his Kingdom fail,
> Swindges the scaly Horrour of his foulded tail.

From this tremendous alexandrine we pass to the proofs
of the new dispensation—the silent oracles, the affrighted
flamens, and the departure of the old gods, fleeing like
ghosts at sunrise, or as

> the yellow-skirted *Fayes*,
> Fly after the Night-steeds, leaving their Moon-lov'd maze.

Finally, in the last stanza, Milton links the Hymn to the introduction by referring again to the guardian angels—

> Bright-harnest Angels sit in order serviceable.

By this means the Nativity becomes a timeless event, belonging to the present as well as to the past.

The poem, youthful as it is, is masterly in its organization, what Dr. Tillyard calls its 'architectonic grasp'; and its bright colouring and vivid pictorial effects are as remarkable as its varied music. It is not surprising that it was Dylan Thomas's favourite poem, or that Keats admired the lovely nineteenth stanza, and remembered it when he wrote his 'Ode to Psyche':

> The Oracles are dumm,
> No voice or hideous humm
>   Runs through the arched roof in words deceiving.
> *Apollo* from his shrine
> Can no more divine,
>   With hollow shreik the steep of Delphos leaving.
> No nightly trance, or breathed spell,
> Inspires the pale-ey'd Priest from the prophetic cell.

The poem uses classical mythology and subsumes it to a Christian purpose; in its brilliance and its occasional tenderness it reveals the Renaissance Milton unspoilt and unequalled.

His immaturity, however, was made apparent by the complete failure of 'The Passion', a subject clearly beyond his range, and his subsequent modest aims in 'On May Morning' and the 'Epitaph on the Marchioness of Winchester'. 'L'Allegro' and 'Il Penseroso' are written, except for the introductions, in the same exquisitely-managed octosyllabic couplets as the 'Epitaph'; but Milton was able to put more of himself into these twin masterpieces. Dr. Tillyard links them with the first of the prolusions, and many critics think that Milton wrote

them before his retirement to the country. It is difficult,
however, to accept Dr. Tillyard's theory that the opening lines of 'L'Allegro', with the fantastic genealogy of
Melancholy,

> Of *Cerberus*, and blackest Midnight born

are meant to be funny, though they are intentionally
grotesque, or his argument that the real contrast is not
between cheerful and melancholy, but between day and
night. Day and night are merely used as appropriate
backgrounds for the contrasting types. Although many
critics have echoed with approval Johnson's criticism of
the poems that they are too little contrasted, that the
cheerful man and the meditative man are too much alike,
there is little substance in the complaint. For Milton is
here contrasting, not the Cavalier with the Puritan way
of life, but rather the two sides of his own character. The
discipline of the prolusion, it is true, had accustomed
Milton to giving the devil his due; but in these poems he
praises in turn the two ways of life which could satisfy
him as a poet and as a man. In both he praises the
pleasures of nature, of drama, and of music; and though
for purposes of argument he segregates the singing of
lark and nightingale, Shakespeare's comedies from 'gorgeous Tragedy In Scepter'd Pall', and 'soft *Lydian* Aires'
from the music of the 'pealing Organ', he himself enjoyed all the pleasures mentioned in both poems—even
the

> Quips and Cranks, and wanton Wiles,
> Nods and Becks, and Wreathed Smiles . . .
> Sport that wrincled Care derides,
> And Laughter holding both his sides.

He implies that the complete man will be a synthesis of
'L'Allegro' and 'Il Penseroso', and we find in these poems
the dialectical method he was afterwards to use so

superbly in *Comus*. Milton in 'L'Allegro' shows how to prevent the pleasurable melancholy of 'Il Penseroso' from turning into melancholia.[1]

Some critics have complained that Milton saw nature through the spectacles of books and that he is inaccurate in some of his descriptions. Mr. Eliot goes further and complains that Milton was deficient in visual imagination and that his sensuousness had been 'withered early by book-learning'. It is true that his descriptions of nature are mostly generalized, and that he combines direct observation with literary associations. He calls the nightingale 'most musicall, most melancholy', and assumes the songster is the female, because he was recalling the legend of Tereus and Philomel. Shakespeare and other great poets have been similarly guilty. But most of the alleged mistakes in Milton's natural history rest on palpable misinterpretations. He does not assert, for example, that the lark comes to his window to bid good-morrow: it is the cheerful man who goes to his window to say good-morrow to the dawn. The other notorious passage, in *Comus*, can also be defended.

> Ere morrow wake, or the low-roosted lark
> From her thatch't pallat rowse . . .

One commentator complains that 'the ideas belong rather to a henhouse than to the resting-place of the lark, which has no thatch over it . . . and, it being on the ground, he does not roost'. But *roosted* merely means *rested*, and *thatched* refers to the composition of the nest: it does not imply a roof.

Milton does not describe what he sees. He depicts a generalized landscape by an accretion of detail from different sources. His spring morning is not a particular morning, any more than the public house in *The Waste*

[1] Cf. J. B. Leishman, *Essays and Studies* (1951), p. 14.

Land is a particular pub. It is curious that Mr. Eliot
should object to Milton's use of a method he frequently
employs himself. 'L'Allegro' and 'Il Penseroso' also
provide several good examples of Milton's use of literary
allusion—another of Mr. Eliot's favourite methods. It
has been suggested by Mr. J. B. Leishman that the two
poems originated in Fletcher's popular song, 'Hence, all
you vaine Delights' and William Strode's reply 'Return
my joyes and hither bring'. In 'L'Allegro' Milton recalls
a passage from one of Marston's satires:

> Dull sprighted *Melancholy*, leaue my braine
> To hell *Cimerian* night, in liuely vaine
> I striue to paint, then hence all darke intent
> And sullen frownes, come sporting meriment,
> Cheeke-dimpling laughter . . .

Compare Milton's lines:

> Hence loathed Melancholy . . .
>
> In dark Cimmerian desert ever dwell . . .
>
> But com thou Goddess fair and free . . .
>
> >Wreathed Smiles
> Such as hang on *Hebe's* cheek
> And love to live in dimple sleek; . . .
>
> And Laughter holding both his sides.

The point of this echo is that Marston's *Scourge of Villanie*
is a representative of the fashionable melancholy of the
late Elizabethans, enshrined in Burton's monumental
Anatomy of Melancholy—and Milton wished to indicate that
he was dismissing an epoch as well as a state of mind. In
'Il Penseroso' he similarly echoes the introductory verses
to the recently published *Anatomy of Melancholy*.

One other example of literary allusion may be given.
The lines in 'Il Penseroso',

As thick and numberless
As the gay motes that people the Sun Beams,

are derived from Chaucer's line, in the Wife of Bath's Tale, referring to the numerous friars

As thikke as motes in the sonne-beem

by whose prayers the faeries have been banished.

As Mr. Leishman has said:[1]

All his materials, one might almost say, lay ready to his hand, and his whole art and power consists in his judicious selection and combination of them. The observance of *decorum*, the subordination of the parts to the whole, the placing of words in a line, of lines in a passage, of passages in a poem—nowhere, perhaps, is that sheer craftsmanship which is the foundation of all great poetry so apparent as in *L'Allegro* and *Il Penseroso*. Almost everything that is commonly understood by 'originality', almost everything that Carew meant when he praised the originality of Donne, is missing: Milton's originality in these two poems consists almost entirely in his manipulation and craftsmanship—in his style, which 'by certain vital signs it had, was likely to live'.

Milton's next poem was the sonnet, discussed in the previous chapter, in which he resolved to live

As ever in my great Taskmaster's eye.

But 'Arcades' was not so much the first-fruit of Milton's new resolve as the result of an invitation, conveyed to him either because of his 'Epitaph on the Marchioness of Winchester' or on the suggestion of Henry Lawes, to write part of an entertainment to be presented before the Countess Dowager of Derby at Harefield. She was an imposing and historic figure: she had been Spenser's patron forty years before this, and her husband had been an early patron of Shakespeare's company. 'Arcades' is a

[1] *Essays and Studies* (1951), pp. 35–6.

charming piece in which Milton had no difficulty in providing what was required: indeed he surpassed all previous pastoral entertainments. It consists of three exquisite songs and a speech in rhymed couplets which gives expression to the idea, already twice used by Milton, that we cannot hear the music of the spheres because of our sin:

> the heavenly tune, which none can hear
> Of human mould with gross unpurged ear.

It is remarkable with what tact and propriety Milton introduced his courtly compliments to his aristocratic patron—only a few years before the struggle between King and Parliament compelled everyone to take sides:

> Nymphs and Shepherds dance no more
>   By sandy *Ladons* Lillied banks . . .
> Here ye shall have greater grace,
> To serve the Lady of this place.

In his next three poems, in which his Taskmaster's eye was more apparent, Milton experimented with a new form, suggested perhaps by Spenser's *Epithalamion* or by Italian *canzoni*, of rhymed verse with lines of irregular length. Sense and rhythmical impetus are prolonged through a whole paragraph, and in this respect the three poems are closer in style (in spite of the rhyme) to *Paradise Lost* than they are to *Comus*. There are only two sentences in the poem 'On Time', and the first sentence of 'At a Solemn Musick' takes up twenty-four lines. 'Upon the Circumcision' is not quite on the same level poetically,[1] but both the other poems are beautifully constructed. One of them works up to a tremendous climax in the final alexandrine—

Triumphing over Death, and Chance, and thee O Time.

[1] Ants Oras has shown (*Notes and Queries*, 1952, pp. 314–15) that the two stanzas of this poem are scrupulously alike and almost identical with one used in one of Tasso's religious *Canzoni*.

The climax of the other is in the short sixteenth line ('Singing everlastingly') and this is followed by a quieter passage describing how

> disproportion'd sin
> Jarr'd against natures chime.

That this metrical virtuosity was not achieved without considerable pains can be seen from the Trinity College manuscript in which there are two rough drafts, very few lines appearing in the first draft in the same form as that of the printed text.

The success of 'Arcades' and Milton's acquaintance with Lawes led, as we have seen, to an invitation to write another masque, this time to celebrate the inauguration of the Earl of Bridgewater as the Lord President of Wales. Lawes wrote the music and played the part of the Attendant Spirit, and the parts of the Lady and her brothers were taken by the Earl's children when the *Mask* (as Milton called it) was performed at Ludlow Castle in September 1634, a date which has been described by G. M. Trevelyan as the high-water mark of English culture.

Comus differs considerably from the traditional court masque in which singing, dancing, and spectacle (to Ben Jonson's annoyance) were more important to the audience than the poetry. A longer entertainment was apparently required for the occasion and Milton ingeniously blended the masque form with that of the pastoral play. For a plot he went to Peele's *Old Wives' Tale* and Fletcher's *Faithful Shepherdess*; his chief character is based (we are told) on Puteanus's Comus; and his theme is derived partly from Jonson's *Pleasure Reconciled to Virtue* in which the leading character is also called Comus. Milton may also have witnessed, or heard about, William Browne's *Circe*.

There is some disagreement amongst the critics about the way *Comus* should be interpreted, and many of them have displayed imperfect sympathies. It has been judged as a masque, and condemned because it violates the conventional expectations: and it has been considered as a play, and ridiculed because of its deficiencies as a drama. Some modern critics have found it hard to stomach the views on chastity and virginity expressed in the poem. Milton's chastity, wrote Herford, 'is at bottom a self-regarding virtue'. Wyndham Lewis, more emphatically, asserted that 'Milton has succeeded in making of what he calls chastity something obscene'. Sir Walter Greg was horrified at the thought that the Lady's speeches were originally recited by a girl of thirteen:

> Milton has deliberately penned passages of self-conceit upon a subject whose delicacy he was apparently incapable of appreciating, and these passages he has placed, to be spoken in her own person, in the mouth of a child just passing into the first dawn of adolescence, thereby outraging at once the innocence of childhood and the reticence of youth.

These attacks on the poet are somewhat unreasonable. Lady Alice's modesty was in fact protected by two substantial cuts in the acting version, and there is no reason to suspect that she, at the age of Juliet when she met Romeo, possessed a fugitive and cloistered virtue. More important is the accusation that Milton's views on chastity were morbid. It is difficult for some people to-day to admire the Lady's militant virginity, especially those who would sympathise with the girl in Graham Greene's *England Made Me*, who replies to the accusation that she is a virgin by slapping the hero's face and exclaiming, 'It was a beastly thing to say'. The Lady and her brothers appear to the modern reader to be a trifle priggish.

Dr. Tillyard has sought to counter this criticism by suggesting that it was later shared by Milton himself, and

that between 1634 and 1637 he realized that the truth
lay neither with Comus nor with the Lady:

> Comus advocates incontinence. The Lady advocates abstin-
> ence. The Attendant Spirit [in the lines on the Garden of
> Adonis] gives the solution, advocating the Aristotelian
> middle course, which for the Lady is the right one; and it is
> marriage.

But it is by no means certain that the Attendant Spirit
does refer to marriage in the Epilogue—it depends on our
interpretation of *The Faerie Queene* to which the lines
refer—and it seems more probable that he was speaking
of what Mr. J. C. Maxwell calls 'the realm where Love
can beget Youth and Joy on the human soul', as in the
Apology for Smectymnuus Love begets on the soul knowledge and virtue. In *Comus* Milton prefaces the passage
with the line

> List mortals, if your ears be true;

and in the *Apology* he adds: 'it might be worth your listen-
ing, readers.'

In the *Apology*, which is vital to the understanding of
Milton's development and in which he was defending
himself against charges of unchastity, he described the
virtues of continence, chastity and virginity in ascending
order of value. He could read with profit

> even those books which to many others have been the fuel
> of wantonness and loose living.

Later he was led

> to the shady spaces of philosophy, but chiefly to the divine
> volumes of Plato, and his equal Xenophon

in whose writings he

> learnt of chastity and love, I mean that which is truly so,
> whose charming cup is only virtue, which she bears in her
> hand to those who are worthy.

The rest, he tells us in a parenthesis which reminds us of Comus's cup,

> are cheated with a thick intoxicating potion, which a certain sorceress, the abuser of love's name, carries about.

Finally, in the Bible he studied

> Those chaste and high mysteries, with timeliest care infused. . . . Nor did I slumber over that place, expressing such high rewards of ever accompanying the Lamb, with those celestial songs to others inapprehensible, but not to those who were not defiled with women, which doubtless means fornication; for marriage must not be called a defilement.

Milton by this time was thinking of getting married, and the only question about this passage is whether he was not unconsciously distorting his earlier views in the light of his matrimonial intentions. Saurat thinks that Milton hoped by means of chastity to acquire supernatural powers—the powers of a great religious poet. From Plato he got the idea, expressed in the second prolusion, the 'Ode on the Morning of Christ's Nativity' and 'Arcades', that the music of the spheres could be heard only by those who restrained their brutish desires. In 'At a Solemn Musick' he links the Platonic idea with the song of the blessed mentioned in the *Book of the Revelation* (Chapter XIV); and in 'Lycidas' and the elegy on Diodati, both written after *Comus*, he describes the joys of heaven which Diodati and King share because of their chaste and virginal lives:

> Since thy bright honour, and thy youth unstain'd
> Have equal favour gain'd,
> Since savour of fleshly lust thou ne'er didst know,
> Behold the honours of virginity
> Reserv'd for thee on high;
> Where thou, thy bright brow crown'd with flaming
>   gold,
> Broad umbrage of triumphal palm shall hold,

And evermore as guest
Of that celestial marriage-feast partake;
Where dance and song concent tempestuous make
With harpings of the blest,
When Sion's Rod to phrenzied rapture brings
His high mysterious Rites and Banquetings.

[tr. Walter Skeat]

But these lines occur in a private elegy: the occasion—
and the fact that Milton himself was still unmarried—
excused, and the fact that Diodati was celibate even
demanded, that the poet should stress the compensating
joys of Paradise. But a masque—even a Miltonic masque
—was a social occasion, and whatever his views at the
time such an emphasis would have been inappropriate.
It is probable that Milton went through a period, after
the first performance of *Comus*, in which he became unduly obsessed with the question of virginity. But in the
poem itself, even with the lines added after 1634, there is
little to which the historically-minded reader should take
exception. One has only to compare the poem with *The
Faithful Shepherdess* to see how much healthier on the subject of chastity Milton is than his predecessor. Fletcher's
play is nominally about chastity; but as Pascal remarks,
it is difficult to write chastely on the subject. Fletcher,
however, does not try very hard. He displays, and
expects his audience to share, the sentimental reverence
for chastity expressed by Lucio in *Measure for Measure*, and
he serves up the favourite dish of certain Sunday news-
papers, pornography sugared with morality. Milton's
praise of chastity was at least dignified by personal experience of the virtue he praised.

In what is perhaps the subtlest of recent interpretations
Professor A. S. P. Woodhouse has argued that Milton in
Comus was presenting a series of related virtues: temper-
ance and continence on the natural level, chastity on a

level common to nature and grace, and the doctrine of
virginity which

> belongs exclusively to the order of grace, which in the poem
> it is used to illustrate and even symbolize.

This pattern, as we have seen, was later followed in
Milton's description of his own development in the
Apology for Smectymnuus. Woodhouse further suggests,
though more controversially, that the three scenes of
Comus are allegorical or symbolical. The wild wood represents this world, 'the order of nature, where good and
evil grow up together and must be circumscribed by
reason'; the Palace of Comus represents one of 'those
crises of temptation which abound in the world'; and
Ludlow Town and Castle represent 'the goal of the pil-
grimage and the reward of virtue'. The Sabrina episode,
with the sprinkling of water, drops of 'precious cure',
symbolizes 'an infusion of divine grace'. Woodhouse goes
on to argue, though less convincingly, that in the Epilogue the stages of the argument are recapitulated in
allegorical form, with the pairs of lovers, Venus and
Adonis, Cupid and Psyche, both derived from *The Faerie
Queene* (Book 3), representing the ascent from the natural
world to an area common to nature and grace, and the
final injunction to love virtue, with its first allusion in all
Milton's works to the doctrine of Christian liberty, representing the state of grace:

> Mortals that would follow me,
> Love vertue, she alone is free,
> She can teach you how to clime
> Higher than the Spheary chime;
> Or if Vertue feeble were
> Heav'n it self would stoop to her.

That Milton intended a wider application than chastity
or virginity in these lines can be deduced from the fact
that when he was on his continental tour he copied the

last lines of this passage into an album, with the comment from Horace: 'I change my sky, but not my spirit when I cross the sea.' The doctrine of Christian liberty is implicit throughout the poem. Although we may agree that Milton was writing on more than one level, and that temperance, chastity and virginity form an ascending scale of values from nature to grace, it is important to recognize that these are merely particular examples of virtue.

In the opening speech the Attendant Spirit speaks of 'the crown that Vertue gives . . . to her true Servants' and declares that some aspire

> To lay their just hands on that Golden Key
> That ope's the Palace of Eternity.

In the concluding lines the same spirit enjoins the audience to love virtue. This is the main argument of the masque: and Professor B. A. Wright suggests that the opening speech is in the main a summary of Plato's *Phaedo* and that Milton

> here as elsewhere in the poem, interprets virtue in the genuine platonic sense, identifying it with the rule of reason and with knowledge; chastity is introduced later as the motive of the story that is to illustrate this larger theme of virtue as knowledge and vice as ignorance.

In a sense, therefore, *Comus* is a kind of Platonic dialogue in the guise of a masque. The virtue to be defended in the poem is, from the nature of the story, chastity; and it is defended partly by the supernatural power of virginity, partly by Heaven itself which stoops to defend it, and partly by force of argument. The central situation in *Comus*, as in *Paradise Lost*, *Paradise Regain'd* and *Samson Agonistes*, is a temptation, and the great debate between Comus and the Lady, prepared for as it is by the prologue and the discussion between the two brothers, is the climax of the poem. In some ways it may be regarded as

D

a debate between two ways of life, the Cavalier and the Puritan, as seen through Puritan eyes—and this was brought out in the Helpmann ballet in which Comus's rout were dressed as cavaliers. It is worth recalling that in an entertainment by another Cambridge poet, Thomas Randolph, whose poems were possibly bound up with a lost edition of *Comus*, there is a defence of fertility not unlike Comus's. But this speech, in *The Muse's Looking-Glass*, was apparently written to express the views of the author:

> Nature has been bountiful
> To provide pleasures, and shall we be niggards
> At plenteous boards? . . .
> . . . Not to enjoy
> All pleasures and at full, were to make Nature
> Guilty of that she ne'er was guilty of—
> A vanity in her works.

Although Milton sees the fallacy in this argument, he gives the devil his due and puts into the mouth of his enchanter some of the best poetry in the whole masque. Much of what Comus says is true, but his arguments are vitiated by their evil purpose. His picture of Nature is not untrue, as far as it goes, as indeed the Lady tacitly admits; his perversion lies in his deduction from Nature's fertility that man should enjoy himself without restraint, that continence is unnatural, and that sexual enjoyment is an end in itself.

The poetical quality of this speech has led critics to argue that Milton was of Comus's party without knowing it; and certainly the Lady's reply is *poetically* inferior. But every good poet has a lively sense of the bounties of Nature, and there is no reason to think that Milton had any sympathy with the evil in Comus. Nor are there any good grounds for supposing that the views of Comus and the Lady were dialectically opposed and that the truth lay with neither side. In her position in the masque she can only take the stand she does, and we must not assume that she failed to appreciate nature, or that she was unnaturally ascetic. It is true that she invokes Faith, Hope and Chastity, instead of the usual Christian Graces; but this was not inserted, as a critic has suggested, to indicate the limitations of her virtue. Chastity is not contrasted with wedded love. For Milton chastity and love went together.

In Jonson's *Pleasure Reconciled to Virtue* pleasure is merely a temporary interlude in a strenuous life. Jonson attempts the reconciliation by the symbol of the dance and by a union of beauty and virtue:

> For what is noble should be sweet
> But not dissolved in wantonness.

But Milton's reconciliation is more profound. Joy is not an interlude—it is the reward of virtue here on earth. 'He repudiates false pleasures, but not joy', remarks Woodhouse. Among the rewards of the virtuous are 'the very things that the adversary would declare to be taken away'. The masque ends appropriately with music and dancing, and with the virtuous brought

> To triumph in victorious dance
> O're sensual Folly, and Intemperance.

There is nothing narrowly puritanical in the conclusion.

Comus in its way is a masterpiece, as it is certainly the greatest of all masques and pastoral plays. Of course, as Johnson complained, 'as a drama it is deficient', and it was easy for him to poke fun at the behaviour of the brothers. But Milton was not writing a drama: he was writing a debate on opposing ways of life in a semi-dramatic form, a study of the rejection of temptation by innocence. It has been called 'a failure in artistic compromise'; but by combining the conventions of the pastoral with those of the masque Milton was able to express

some of his deepest feelings about life, while at the same
time providing his audience with a brilliant entertainment. Lawes, though a royalist, was able to recognize
and eager to advertise the poem's loveliness; and the
veteran Elizabethan poet, Sir Henry Wotton, was
ravished with what he called 'a certain Dorique delicacy'
in the songs and odes 'whereunto I must plainly confess
to have seen yet nothing parallel in our language.' The
praise was genuine, and it has stood the test of time.

Hopkins once remarked, 'The effect of studying masterpieces is to make me admire and do otherwise.'
Milton might have said the same. The blank verse of
Comus, though it owes more to the verse of Shakespeare's
middle period than to that of any other writer, is yet
distinctly Miltonic. Milton felt, rightly, that the blank
verse of his immediate contemporaries had become loose
and flabby. He rejected Massinger, Shirley and Fletcher
as models—though there are echoes of *The Faithful Shepherdess* in the rhymed parts of *Comus*—and returned to the
Elizabethans. His rhythmical unit is normally the line.
There are occasional distant echoes of *A Midsummer-
Night's Dream* and *The Tempest*, and in one passage Milton
seems to recall two speeches in *King Lear*: Lear's own
words—

> Expose thyself to feel what wretches feel,
> That thou mayst shake the superflux to them
> And shew the heavens more just . . .

and Gloucester's—

> Let the superfluous and lust-dieted man . . .
> Feel your power quickly;
> So distribution shall undo excess,
> And each man have enough.

The Lady in *Comus* has a similar thought, but no one could
mistake her lines for Shakespeare's:

If every just man that now pines with want
Had but a moderate and beseeming share
Of that which lewdly-pamper'd Luxury
Now heaps upon som few with vast excess,
Natures full blessings would be well dispenc't
In unsuperfluous eeven proportion,
And she no whit encomber'd with her store,
And then the giver would be better thank't,
His praise due paid, for swinish gluttony
Ne're looks to Heav'n amidst his gorgeous feast,
But with besotted base ingratitude
Cramms, and blasphemes his feeder.

Apart from the difference of versification, it may be noted that Shakespeare's characters are concerned more with the needs of the poor (not necessarily of the deserving poor) than with the evils of gluttony; but the Lady—and her lines are in character—is more concerned with the vices of the rich and with the virtue of temperance. Her redistribution of wealth would assist only the *just* man who pines with want. Lear arraigns the justice of the heavens; Milton, typically, blames the vices of men.

That Milton's avoidance of the style of contemporary dramatists was deliberate can be seen from an examination of the manuscript of *Comus*, which contains passages more akin to the work of the Jacobeans than anything in the printed text. In the manuscript, for example, the Elder Brother declares:

I do not, brother,
Infer, as if I thought my sisters state
Secure without all doubt or question, no
I could be willing though now i'the darke to trie
A tough passado with the shaggiest ruffian
That lurks by hedge or lane of this dead circuit
To have her by my side, though I were sure
She might be free from perill where she is.

Milton soon changed the surprising *passado* to the more

decorous *encounter*; but the last six lines appeared in the
acting version and were deleted only between the performance and the masque's publication. He rightly
judged that the diction of the passage was out of keeping
with the necessary artificiality of the masque form.

Comus was published with a Virgilian epigraph, bewail-
ing that the poet had let the sirocco of publicity breathe
on his tender flowers. *Lycidas*, in the following year,
opened with an echo of the same lament:

> Yet once more, O ye Laurels, and once more
> Ye Myrtles brown, with Ivy never-sear,
> I com to pluck your Berries harsh and crude,
> And with forc'd fingers rude,
> Shatter your leaves before the mellowing year.

The extent of Milton's ambition can be gauged from the
modest way in which he speaks of his own early master-
pieces.

According to Milton's nephew, there always existed
between Edward King and the poet 'a particular friend-
ship and intimacy'. King, a fellow of Milton's college,
was only twenty-five when he was drowned in the Irish
Sea on 10 August, 1637. Milton wrote *Lycidas* in November of the same year, and it was included in a volume of
memorial poems, in Greek, Latin, and English, published
in the following year. Many of the contributors were
fellows or graduates of Christ's College. Most of them
were scholars rather than poets, though Joseph Beaumont
is well known as the author of *Psyche* and a posthumous
collection of religious poems, Henry More was the
famous poetic Platonist, and Cleveland was a royalist, and
a minor metaphysical of some talent and little taste. He
produced an extravagant effusion which advertises his
own cleverness and throws doubt on the genuineness of
his grief:

I am no Poet here; my penne's the spout
Where the rain-water of my eyes run out
In pitie of that name, whose fate we see
Thus copi'd out in griefs Hydrographie . . .
When we have fill'd the rundlets of our eyes,
We'll issue't forth and vent such elegies,
As that our tears shall seem the Irish seas,
We floating Islands, living Hebrides.

Milton's poem, over the initials J.M., is the last poem
in the volume; and it is to be hoped that the editor
realized, even if the reading-public preferred Cleveland's
fustian, that *Lycidas* belonged to a different order of
poetry. It has been attacked for its insincerity. Johnson
could not believe that a man who was genuinely grieving
for a friend would produce a poem in such a stale and
conventional form as the pastoral elegy. He compared,
to Milton's disadvantage, the prosaic straightforwardness
of Cowley's elegy on Harvey; and later critics have contrasted the manly sincerity of Johnson's own verses in
memory of a friend. But although the pastoral in the
seventeenth and eighteenth centuries was often frigid and
tedious, it had been used by good poets in many languages
and it was to be used effectively after Johnson's death by
Shelley and Arnold. Milton was writing within a long and
honourable tradition, and even the intrusion of 'most
awful and sacred truths' had the precedent of Spenser, to
go no further. The artificiality of the convention was not
necessarily a disadvantage. It was a means of objectifying
the emotions expressed, and of preventing the personal
feeling from swamping the poetry. Whether Milton was
a close friend of King or not is irrelevant, partly because
a funeral elegy requires a certain detachment—it is
public, formal, ceremonial—and partly because King is
merely the nominal subject of the poem. Scholars have
listed the subjects traditionally treated in the pastoral

form by Mantuan, Spenser and others, and shown that Milton drags every one of them into *Lycidas*, which is a kind of epitome of the form. Considered in the light of the tradition, even the much-criticized attack on the clergy is a perfectly legitimate theme. It cannot be regarded even as a digression, since the high-minded disinterestedness of King (though he secured his fellowship by political influence) and his genuine piety could properly be contrasted with the corruption of the bad shepherds. It is, indeed, a passage which serves to lift the pastoral form to a higher level. It may be conventional for Milton to talk of shepherds driving their flocks, when all he means is that they were undergraduates together; but the Biblical associations of sheep and shepherd, the injunction to St. Peter, 'Feed my lambs', and the derivative meaning of 'pastor' enable the poet to teach parabolically without the intrusion of direct didacticism and without shattering the conventions.

Johnson objected not merely to the pastoral convention, but also to the diction which he said was 'harsh, the rhymes uncertain, and the numbers unpleasing.' He may have meant by 'harsh' repugnant to the understanding, as his defenders have urged; but he is more likely to have been referring to the deliberate harshness of such lines as

Grate on their scrannel Pipes of wretched straw,

to the occasional short lines, to the varying lengths of paragraphs and the varying position of the rhyme, and above all to the presence of some dozen unrhymed lines. All these were the common practice of contemporary Italian poets who, rather than Petrarch or Spenser, served as Milton's models. Miss Gretchen Finney has argued persuasively[1] that Milton's monody was influenced in certain details of form, structure and content by Italian

[1] *Huntington Library Quarterly*, XV, 325 ff.

musical dramas, especially by Striggio's libretto for Monteverdi's *La favola d'Orfeo* and Stefano Landi's *Morte
d'Orfeo*. The Orpheus myth is obviously central to the
poem. There were English models too. Giles and
Phineas Fletcher were admired poets at Cambridge and
the last part of *Christ's Victory and Triumph* and the end of
The Purple Island provided material for the passage
describing the joys of heaven in *Lycidas*. Milton also
imitated *The Purple Island*, it has been suggested, in his
description of ambition, in his account of the death of
Orpheus, and in his concluding lines which resemble
these of Fletcher:

> But see, the stealing night with softly pace,
> To flie the western sunne, creeps up the east;
> Cold Hesper 'gins unmask his evening face,
> And calls the winking starres from drouzie rest:
> Home then my lambes; the falling drops eschew;
> To morrow shall ye feast in pastures new,
> And with the rising sunne banquet on pearled dew.

There is some slight evidence that Milton also laid under
contribution Browne's elegy on Philarete in *The Shepherd's Pipe*. It is worth mentioning these echoes not in
order to demonstrate that *Lycidas* is essentially derivative
and conventional, but to show that Milton's method of
allusion is not unlike Eliot's, who remarks that in reading a great poet one is always conscious of his predecessors. Milton does not slavishly imitate; in *Lycidas* he invariably improves on what he borrows, and the total
effect is infinitely more powerful than Browne or the
Fletchers ever achieved. Its diction is throughout exquisite, the placing of the rhymes so skilful that the unrhymed lines pass unnoticed or as subtle discords, and
the metre varied enough to express the contrasts of the
poem without straining its form.

Lycidas is the crown of English pastoral poetry: the

artificiality of the form is burned up by the passionate sincerity of the poet. Milton turned a *pièce d'occasion* into a soul-searching examination of his poetic ambitions; for the real subject, of course, is not Edward King but John Milton. He debates with himself on the subject of unfulfilled renown: but for the grace of God, he thinks, he might be drowned on his forthcoming voyage to France:

> So may som gentle Muse
> With lucky words favour my destin'd Urn . . .
> For we were nurst upon the self-same hill,
> Fed the same flock, by fountain, shade, and rill.

The climax of the first part of the poem is when Milton recalls the inability of the muse to save Orpheus,

> When by the rout that made the hideous roar,
> His goary visage down the stream was sent,
> Down the swift *Hebrus* to the *Lesbian* shore.

To be a poet does not protect one against premature death; and Milton asks if the austerity of his dedication and of his thirty years' apprenticeship was not a waste of time:

> Were it not better done as others use,
> To sport with *Amaryllis* in the shade,
> Or with the tangles of *Neæra's* hair?

He is comforted by Phoebus, who tells him that unfulfilled promise does not preclude 'fame in heaven'. But Milton's doubts return. The shipwreck took place in a calm sea; and King's death seemed unfair and wasteful, for St. Peter himself admits that the dead man was a devoted cleric, in contrast to the 'corrupted clergy, then in their height'. There follows the lovely passage describing the strewing of imaginary flowers on the 'Laureat Herse'. Botanically minded critics have pointed out that all the eleven flowers would be dead by the time Milton wrote the poem; but as the poet admits that he is dallying with false surmise, any burial being impossible, the criticism is otiose. In the final section of the poem Milton resolves the problems which had obsessed him. He is consoled for his fears of early death by the prospect of immortality; his fears for the future of the Church are compensated by the 'solemn troops and sweet Societies' of the saints in heaven; and his agonizing desire for fame is succeeded by trust in God. Dr. Tillyard even suggests that Milton renounces earthly fame, and that there is an 'abnegation of self by the great egotist'. But, if this is true, the abnegation was only temporary.[1]

Although we are concerned mainly with Milton as an English poet, it is important to remember that nearly half his early poems were written in Latin, that it was these that impressed the Italian intellectuals, and that apart from the intrinsic merits of two or three of them, they are interesting from the biographical point of view. Johnson quoted with approval the verdict of Hampton that 'Milton was the first Englishman who, after the revival of letters, wrote Latin verses with classic elegance'; Coleridge remarked that if the poems had come to us as written in the age of Tiberius we should have thought them very beautiful; and Mark Pattison declared that Milton stood alone in being able to 'give utterance to genuine passion' in such exercises. The first ten of these poems, however, written during Milton's first years at Cambridge, are merely competent but uninspired exercises. The one on the Gunpowder Plot, because of its links with *Paradise Lost*, has probably been overpraised. But, taken as a whole, these poems show

[1] Apart from books listed in the bibliography the following articles on the early poems may be consulted: A. S. P. Woodhouse, *University of Toronto Quarterly*, XI, 46–71; XIX, 218–23. J. C. Maxwell, *The Cambridge Journal*, I, 376–80. J. H. Hanford, 'The Youth of Milton' in *Studies in Shakespeare, Milton and Donne* (1925). C. S. Lewis, *The Review of English Studies* (1932), pp. 170–6. J. B. Leishman, *Essays and Studies* (1951). Charles Williams, Preface to the World's Classics Milton (1940).

at least that Milton developed earlier as a writer of Latin
verse than he did as an English poet; and his first masterpiece, *In adventum veris*, was written eight months before
the Nativity Ode. This poem, indeed, is particularly interesting, since it extends our knowledge of Milton's
range. Compared with the May morning song, written
a year later, the Latin poem is sensuous and uninhibited.
Inspired partly by the season, and more perhaps by Ovid,
Milton indulges in what has been called his *Sacre du Prin-
temps*. The lines near the beginning, describing the
nightingale, are closely linked with Milton's first sonnet:

> Nightingale darkling in the small new leaves,
>   Warbling thy song when all the woods are still,
> I in the town shall sing beneath the eaves,
>   Thou in the tree-tops singing all thy will.
>
> Hail to him, hail to him, once again returning,
>   Hail to our lord the Spring, all hail we cry.
> Keep we his feast, when the year's at the turning,
>   Sing we his song, the nightingale and I.
>
> [tr. Helen Waddell]

The section of the poem describing the love of the Earth
for the Sun is full of warmth and colour; and the concluding section describes, in lines compared by Dr. Tillyard to Swinburne's famous chorus from *Atalanta in
Calydon*, a riot of sensuality:

> Now in the twilight come the satyrs dancing
>   In nimble bands across the flower-starred meadows;
> Sylvanus, crowned with cypress-leaves, advancing,
>   Half-goat, half-god, amid the falling shadows.
>
> Out from their woods and over the hill-side
>   The Dryads range; Pan riots through the glade,
> That Cybele herself is fain to hide,
>   And even Mother Ceres is afraid.

Faunus an Oread furiously pursues;
    She feigns to hide, her limbs by panic shaken;
But burning for the thing she must refuse:
    She flees, still longing to be overtaken.

> [tr. Kenneth Muir]

It is characteristic of Milton that several of his Latin poems should discuss his poetic plans. In the lines addressed to his father, he speaks in general terms of his ambitions, which include accompanying his own songs in heaven, 'wherewith the stars and the arch of heaven shall resound'. In the poem written to Manso he writes more specifically of an epic on a British subject:

If ever I should sing my native kings,
And Arthur waging war beneath the earth,
If ever I sing the Knights of the Table Round,
And, with the spirit's aid, the shattering
Of Saxon phalanxes by British arms . . .

> [tr. Kenneth Muir]

In the *Epitaph on Damon* he again indicates that he will choose a British theme;

For I would tell
Of Trojan ships on the Rutupian Sea,
Of Imogen's old realm—Pandrasus' daughter—
Of famous princes, Brennus, old Belinus,
And Arviragus, of British colonists
In western Gaul; then would I tell of Igraine,
Pregnant with Arthur by a fatal fraud,
For with the seeming face of Gorloïs
Came Uther to her bed by Merlin's art . . .
Why not a British theme?

> [tr. Kenneth Muir]

The *Epitaph* is the most impressive of the Latin poems, and in the opinion of many critics it is worthy to rank with *Lycidas*. But although the sorrow it expresses may be more personal, it is in many ways a more conventional pastoral than the English poems. Apart from the final ecstatic section in which the poet writes of the joys of heaven (quoted on p. 36) the most notable passages in the poem are those which describe the poet's loneliness at being deprived of the one friend to whom he could open his heart:

> To whom now shall I turn? who now will teach
> My heart to blunt its gnawing cares, and cheat
> The night with friendly talk, while juicy pears
> Hiss by the fire, and chestnuts on the hearth
> Crack open, while the wild tempestuous wind
> Turns all to chaos, roaring in the elms.

> Alone I wander in the fields, alone
> Through pastures green; and where the trees grow thick
> Down in the valleys, I await the dusk,
> While the rain falls on me and the wind moans,
> And the woodland shade is flecked with gleams of light.
> [tr. Kenneth Muir]

Milton's Latin poems are not without faults: he is some-times guilty of false quantities, his meaning is not always clear, and he took a long time to free himself from the taint of the poetic exercise. But at their best, the Latin poems are worthy to stand beside the English poems of the 1645 volume.

Chapter Four

MARRIAGE AND WARFARE

'To-morrow to fresh woods and pastures new.'
It has been suggested by Hanford that the death
of Milton's mother and Christopher's coming to live at
Horton may have spurred on the poet to complete his
education by taking a long-projected tour of the con-
tinent. Armed with advice and letters of introduction
from Sir Thomas Wotton he left England in May accompanied by one servant and was received by the English
Ambassador in Paris, who gave him an introduction to
Hugo Grotius, the famous scholar who was the Swedish
ambassador in Paris. Milton would have been interested
in his plan for uniting the Protestant Churches of
Europe, and perhaps in his Latin play, *Adamus Exul*. He
travelled through France to Nice, sailed from there to
Genoa, and arrived at Florence, where he stayed about
two months. He became intimate with many persons of
rank and learning, as he tells us, and attended the meetings of literary academies. The minutes of one academy
record that Milton 'read a very learned Latin poem in
hexameters'. According to the poet's account his
juvenilia were received with 'written encomiums' and
this account is corroborated by the commendatory verses
from his Italian friends he prefixed to his Latin poems
when they were published in 1645. The friends included
Carlo Dati, a boy of nineteen, who kept up a correspondence with him for some years, Jacopo Gaddi, poet
and patron, and Antonio Malatesti, who dedicated to
Milton a sonnet-sequence entitled *La Tina*.

During his stay at Florence, Milton made an expedition
to a place that he was to remember twenty years later—

> the Brooks
> In *Vallombrosa*, where th'*Etrurian* shades
> High overarch't imbowr.

He also paid a visit, either now or on his return to
Florence, to Galileo, old, blind, ill, and under the sur-
veillance of the Inquisition. He may have had a letter of
introduction from Carlo Dati, who had been Galileo's
pupil, from Elia Diodati, a relative of Milton's friend, or
from Grotius. We do not know how Milton obtained
permission to visit the old astronomer, unless it was from
Cardinal Barberini whom he was later to meet in Rome.
In any case the visit made a deep impression on his mind,
and he referred to it in his plea for unlicensed printing.

About the beginning of October Milton continued his
journey to Siena and Rome. Here he spent most of his
time in viewing the antiquities, but he dined at the
English Jesuit College—in spite of his bitter attack on
the Society of Jesus in his early poem on the Gunpowder
Plot—and he took up some introductions given him by
his new Florentine friends. After two months in Rome
he passed on to Naples, where he met Giovanni Baptista
Manso, Marquis of Villa. The poet was delighted to have
the chance of making the acquaintance of the patron, the
friend, and the biographer of the great Tasso. Manso in
his old age was devout, and he lamented that Milton's
creed was not worthy of his beauty, his intelligence, and
his morals:

> Ut mens, forma, decor, facies, mos, si pietas sic,
> Non Anglus, verum hercle Angelus ipse fores.

But in spite of the difference of religion Manso showed
Milton much kindness and presented him with two of his
own books—cups, as Milton pastorally called them in his

Epitaphium Damonis—and the poet wrote *Mansus* in honour of his new acquaintance.

After staying a few weeks in Naples, Milton was about to cross over into Sicily and Greece when he received news from England which made him alter his plans. Charles I's attempt to force the English prayer-book on Scotland and his preparations for invasion alarmed and shocked the English Puritans, and Milton (as he tells us) 'thought it base to be travelling for amusement abroad, while my fellow-citizens were fighting at home.' But although he gave up his longed-for visit to Greece he took seven or eight months to reach England. As he started back to Rome he was told by some merchants that the English Jesuits had formed a plot against him if he returned to Rome, because he had spoken too freely about religion.

He tells us himself

> For I had laid it down as a rule for myself never to begin a conversation on religion in those parts, but if interrogated concerning my faith, whatever might be the consequence, to dissemble nothing.

He may, in retrospect, have exaggerated the danger; but there is no reason to suppose that he invented it in order to advertise his own bravery. Doubtless the merchants unintentionally misled him. But, in any case, in spite of their warning he returned to Rome, and 'defended, as before, the orthodox faith, for nearly two months more, even in the city of the sovereign pontiff himself.' He met the Vatican Librarian, Holsten, and was by him introduced to Cardinal Barberini. He attended a performance of a comic opera in the Cardinal's private theatre, and he wrote a series of epigrams on a singer, Leonora Baroni, who had a wide circle of poetical admirers.

Milton went to Florence early in March, where he again attended meetings of one of the literary academies.

E

From thence he moved on to Venice, where he packed up the books he had acquired on his travels—including some of Monteverdi's music. He passed through Verona and Milan on the way to Geneva, where Charles Diodati's uncle, a well-known theologian, lived. He must have heard then, if not before, of the death of Charles Diodati in August 1638. Milton returned to England, probably by the beginning of August 1639. Johnson sneers at the spectacle of Milton hurrying home to take part in the struggle for liberty only to set up as a schoolmaster to his nephews, Edward and John Phillips, whose mother had remarried. After a short while in lodgings Milton acquired a secluded house with a garden in Aldersgate Street. Both the boys boarded with him, and later on he took more pupils. Milton mentions only that he acquired a house for himself and his books, and that he delightedly resumed his studies. His teaching he regarded as incidental to his main pursuits, and he had not yet had a clear call to intervene in political controversy: Charles I had not yet been induced to call a parliament. Fresh from the excitement of meeting the Italian intellectuals, and kindled by their praises of his own immature works, Milton was anxious to compose the great poetry for which his long apprenticeship had fitted him. His mind was filled with schemes for epics and tragedies, and he wished also to write works of scholarship. One of these, *A Perfect System of Divinity*, afterwards became his treatise on *Christian Doctrine*. He made use of his pupils for this work by getting them to read books he needed, by expounding the Greek Testament to them, and by dictating to them parts of his treatise.

Milton's educational theories, later to be outlined in his tractate *Of Education*, were not intended for the average boy; but they might be more suitable for the training of an intellectual aristocracy. Milton wanted to

design an education to fit a man 'to perform justly, skil-
fully, and magnanimously all the offices, public and
private, of peace and war.' He wanted it to repair the
ill effects of the Fall. It was to include the study of
languages, not for their own sake, but for the wisdom
and knowledge to be found written in them. It was to
include the study of rhetoric, mathematics and the
sciences, agriculture (in classical treatises) and a huge
range of classical authors, theology, history, and politics.
For recreation they would read plays in Greek, Latin and
Italian, and poetry in various languages, 'as being less
subtle and fine' than rhetoric, 'but more simple, sensuous and passionate'. The pupils would have plenty of
exercise—fencing, wrestling—and while they were un-
sweating themselves they would listen to 'solemn and
divine harmonies of music.' The average pupil would
have floundered in the early stages of this ambitious programme, and one of Milton's asides ('And either now, or
before this, they may have easily learned at any odd hour
the Italian tongue') shows how little he understood what
ordinary boys were like. His essay was doubtless based
on his practice, though his results must often have been
disappointing. Naturally enough, in accordance with the
disciplinary views of the time, he did not spare the rod;
and the first Mrs. Milton sympathized, we are told, with
the little victims.

Meanwhile, in his *Epitaph on Damon*, the finest of his
Latin poems, Milton had said farewell to Charles Diodati. In it he looks backward to his Italian journey, and
forward to his epic on King Arthur. Instead of the epic,
however, he began a play on the subject of the Fall, perhaps on the model of Andreini's *Adamo*, which he may
have seen performed while he was in Italy. But these
poetical plans were interrupted by the developing political situation.

The Long Parliament met in November 1640, and a month later they were petitioned by the Puritans to abolish episcopacy. At the end of March, the Bishops' Exclusion Bill was introduced to prevent the clergy from holding state employment. Two months later the Root and Branch Bill, to abolish all ecclesiastical orders above the rank of minister, passed its second reading, and was thereafter shelved. In the Grand Remonstrance the Bishops were accused of designing to subvert the fundamental laws and principles of government. These events were accompanied by a pamphlet war, and Milton describes in his *Second Defence* how he came to intervene:

> The vigour of the parliament had begun to humble the pride of the bishops. As soon as the liberty of speech was no longer subject to control, all mouths began to be opened against the bishops; some complained of the vices of the individuals, others of those of the order. They said that it was unjust that they alone should differ from the model of other reformed Churches; that the government of the church should be according to the pattern of other churches, and particularly the word of God.
>
> This awakened all my attention and my zeal. I saw that a way was opening for the establishment of real liberty; that the foundation was laying for the deliverance of man from the yoke of slavery and superstition; that the principles of religion, which were the first objects of our care, would exert a salutary influence on the manners and constitution of the state; and as I had from my youth studied the distinctions between religious and civil rights, I perceived that if I ever wished to be of use I ought at least not to be wanting to my country, to the church, and to so many of my fellow-Christians, in a crisis of so much danger; I therefore determined to relinquish the other pursuits in which I was engaged, and to transfer the whole force of my talents and my industry to this one important object. (F)

Milton did not mention that he had a more personal

motive for engaging in the war of pamphlets. His old
tutor and friend, Thomas Young, had in collaboration
with four others, written a reply to Bishop Hall's defence
of episcopacy. Hall and the Archbishop of Armagh,
James Ussher, had both replied to Smectymnuus (a name
made up of the initials of Young and his friends). At
about the same time Milton published his first pamphlet,
Of Reformation in England; and in the next pamphlets on
episcopacy, written in rapid succession in the summer of
1641, *Of Prelatical Episcopacy* and *Animadversions upon
the Remonstraunt's Defence*, he replied directly to Hall and
Ussher in defence of Young and his friends 'who were
hardly a match for the eloquence of their opponents'.
Hall retorted in one pamphlet, and Milton believed that
he assisted another writer, perhaps one of his sons, in a
violent attack on Milton's morals. Milton replied in *The
Reason of Church Government*, and to the personal attack in
An Apology against a Pamphlet called a Modest Confutation,
better known as the *Apology for Smectymnuus*.

In his first pamphlets Milton, like most of the Par-
liamentarians, was not opposed to the monarchy. Indeed, he professed to attack the Bishops partly because
he felt that their actions weakened the King's authority.
Monarchy, he thought, was compatible with the liberty
of the subject; but the Bishops

> for these many years have not ceast in their Pulpits wrinch-
> ing and spraining the *text*, to set at nought and trample under
> foot all the most sacred, and life-blood Lawes, Statutes and
> Acts of *Parliament*, that are the holy Cov'nant of Union, and
> Marriage between the King and his Realme.

He thought that the British Constitution was essentially
the best in the world, and that the Bishops were busy
undermining it. Even in the last of the pamphlets on
episcopacy, written on the eve of the Civil War, Milton
admits that the King is the Lord's Anointed, though the

Bishops, like Delilah, had wickedly shaved off 'those bright and weighty tresses of his laws and just prerogatives.' He still hoped that with the abolition of the Bishops the King would become a constitutional ruler.

In these years Milton had great faith in the political wisdom and maturity of ordinary men. He believed that the plain artisan was quite competent to arrive at religious truth without assistance. He thought of God as 'a most indulgent father', who directed his sons 'in the sweetest and mildest manner of paternal discipline.' Unlike most of his fellow puritans, Milton spoke tolerantly of sects and heresies, and he exhibited no disdain of innocent pastimes. He even argued that it was the duty of the State to encourage arts and recreations.

Looking back, we can see that Milton's hopes at this time were absurdly Utopian. But he was not alone in thinking that England was entering on a new and glorious age—an age of political freedom and religious truth. England was to reform the Reformation and be an example to Europe. The Kingdom of Heaven was at hand:

> Come therefore O thou that hast the seven starres in thy right hand, appoint thy chosen *Priests* according to their Orders, and courses of old, to minister before thee, and duely to dresse and powre out the consecrated oyle into thy holy and ever-burning lamps; thou hast sent out the spirit of prayer upon thy servants over all the Land to this effect, and stirr'd up their vowes as the sound of many waters about thy Throne. Every one can say that now certainly thou hast visited this Land, and hast not forgotten the utmost corners of the earth, in a time when men had thought that thou wast gone up from us to the farthest end of the Heavens, and hadst left to doe marvellously among the sons of these last Ages. O perfect, and accomplish thy glorious acts; . . . seeing the power of thy grace is not past away with the primitive times, as fond and faithless men imagine, but thy

Kingdome is now at hand, and thou standing at the dore.
Come forth out of thy Royal Chambers, O Prince of all the
Kings of the earth, put on the visible roabes of thy imperiall
Majesty, take up that unlimited Scepter which thy Almighty
Father hath bequeath'd thee; for now the voice of thy Bride
calls thee, and all creatures sigh to bee renew'd.

Sir Herbert Grierson has compared Milton's feelings at
this time with those of Wordsworth at the time of the
French Revolution. He might indeed have said with
Wordsworth

> Bliss was it in that dawn to be alive.

and

> Society became my glittering bride,
> And airy hopes my children.

But it must be admitted that Milton emerged from the
first of his controversies not entirely unscathed. His first
pamphlet was noble and dignified; in the third he
descended to vulgar abuse. There was a 'grim laughter'
mingled with 'the serious uncasing of a grand imposture'.
Milton's natural generosity made him a little uneasy about
his passages of invective, and some of his less partisan
friends apparently protested. He wrote them because he
believed—obtusely, we may think—that they were in
keeping with his theme, that there were classical and
Biblical precedents for them, and because his opponents
employed the same weapons.

In the detecting and convincing of any notorious enemy to
truth and his country's peace . . . I suppose, and more than
suppose, it will be nothing disagreeing from Christian meek-
ness to handle such a one in a rougher accent, and to send
home his haughtiness well besputed with his own holy
water.

This tradition of religious controversy dates back at least
fifty years to the Martin Mar-Prelate struggle, in which

62   *John Milton*

both sides were bitterly satirical; but most modern readers feel that such invective was beneath the dignity of the author of *Comus* and that the resultant hardening of his sensibilities marred his later poetry.

Naturally Bishop Hall, though he had been a satirist in his youth, was incensed; and his son or another replied for him with an attack on Milton's morals, purporting to be based on the evidence of his pamphlets:

> It is like hee spent his youth, in loytering, bezelling, and har-lotting. Thus being grown to an Impostume in the brest of the University, he was at length vomited out thence into a Suburbe sinke about *London*; which, since his comming up, hath groaned under two ills, *Him* and the *Plague*. Where his morning haunts are I wist not; but he that would finde him after dinner, must search the *Play-Houses*, or the *Bordelli*, for there I have traced him.

Milton was disturbed by this imaginary portrait, especially as he had heard that the Halls had made enquiries about his private life and had then drawn on their imaginations for the unsavoury details they could not glean from rumour. The fact that Milton had been rus-ticated and that he did live in a suburb makes it probable that his antagonists knew more about him than they pretended. They also had the bad taste to sneer at the great prayer in *Animadversions upon the Remonstrant's Defence*:

> Though the language be not in it self unknown, yet the harsh-nesse of it in some, the length and tediousnesse of stile in others, the affected heighth of forced Allegories and Tropes, not to say the nonsense and ridiculously absurd variations of many pretenders to the faculty, renders it altogether as un-intelligible, as it were Latine or Greek. If I were to make good this assertion by a particular instance I would go no farther than your prayer . . . which infinite of honest and simple Christians would no more know how to understand than they would doe a Scene out of Jonson's *Cataline*.

Milton retaliated by ridiculing the Bishop's 'toothless' satires, written in the previous century. But we may be grateful that the Halls—if they were indeed responsible —made their libellous attack, for it impelled Milton to write in reply the most illuminating of all his auto-biographical digressions, in which he counters the accusation that he was 'vomited' from the university— possibly a garbled account of his rustication—and that he led an immoral life in a notorious suburb, by describing his Cambridge career, his reading, and his passionate love of chastity.

Milton lamented that he had had to postpone his proper task of writing great poetry to engage in un-pleasant controversy. He had had to leave

> a calme and pleasing solitarynes fed with cheerful and con-fident thoughts, to imbark on a troubl'd sea of noises and hoarse disputes, put from beholding the bright countenance of truth in the quiet and still air of delightfull studies to come into the dim reflexion of hollow antiquities sold by the seeming bulk, and there be fain to club quotations with men whose learning and belief lies in marginal stuffings.

Certainly to the modern reader these anti-episcopacy pamphlets are somewhat indigestible because of the con-troversial method then in vogue of belabouring one's opponent with quotations. Milton speaks scornfully of those who think they have proved their points by stuffing their needless tractates 'with the specious names of Ignatius and Polycarpus'. He himself quotes lavishly, though mainly from the Bible. The practice was in-evitable in a discussion of church government.

Milton felt that verse was his natural medium and that in writing prose he was using only his left hand. But it should not be assumed that he wrote prose merely from a sense of topical duty. He had always been interested in the subjects about which he wrote; and we can find in his commonplace book the evidence of his study of most of the subjects on which he was afterwards to write pamphlets—episcopacy, monarchy, and even divorce. But in 1641, with his mind full of poetical plans, he made a real sacrifice in engaging in controversy; and he disliked what he considered to be his duty. He would have preferred to

> be the messenger of gladnes and contentment . . . but when God commands to take the trumpet and blow a dolorous or a jarring blast, it lies not in mans will what he shall say or what he shall conceal.

In spite of some jarring blasts, Milton remained full of hope and enthusiasm, even though he realized the imminence of war. In the *Apology for Smectymnuus* he describes how he takes exercise to preserve the body's health and hardiness—

> to render lightsome, clear, and not lumpish obedience to the mind, to the cause of religion, and our country's liberty, when it shall require firm hearts in sound bodies to stand and cover their stations, rather than to see the ruin of our protestation, and the inforcement of a slavish life.

Four months later the King raised his standard at Nottingham, and in the meantime Milton had married the daughter of a Royalist.

> About *Whitsuntide* it was, or a little after, that he took a Journey into the Country; no body about him certainly knowing the Reason, or that it was any more than a Journey of Recreation: after a Month's stay, home he returns a Married man, that went out a Batchelor; his wife being *Mary*, the Eldest Daughter of Mr. *Richard Powell*, then a Justice of Peace, of *Forrest-hil*, near *Shotover* in Oxfordshire; some few of her nearest Relations accompanying the Bride to her new Habitation: which by reason the Father nor any body else were yet come, was able to receive them.

Edward Phillips was only twelve years old at the time of his uncle's marriage, and he was writing after the lapse of nearly half a century. It is fairly certain that 1642 rather than 1643 was the date of the marriage, since it would have been nearly impossible after the outbreak of the war; and it is unlikely that Milton would write his first divorce pamphlet on his honeymoon, and not after his wife's desertion. Milton's father, who had been born near Forest Hill, had lent money to Richard Powell some fifteen years before, and the £500 owed to the poet since then was still unpaid. Perhaps Milton went to discuss the payment of the debt, and perhaps Powell thought that if he sacrificed his daughter to his creditor he would not be pressed to pay. Mary was not yet seventeen, her bridegroom being twice her age, and she was 'used to a great House, and much Company and Joviality'. But Milton looked young; he was handsome and pleasing in his manners; he was known to her rather as a poet with aristocratic patrons and a passionate love of music than as the opponent of episcopacy. She was quickly disillusioned. After her relations had sung and danced and feasted in Milton's quiet house, they departed, leaving her to a kind of life for which nothing in her education or her upbringing had fitted her. Milton returned to his studies and his teaching, and from the divorce pamphlets it would seem that he soon found that he and his wife had little in common. Mary, after a month or so of marriage, received an invitation to visit her parents who realized that war was imminent. Milton consented to her departure, but stipulated that she should return by Michaelmas. The weeks passed, and she did not re-appear. Milton wrote letters which were disregarded, and sent a messenger who was 'dismissed with some contempt'. There is no doubt that Mary shared her parents' royalist views, and it is not surprising that in time of war she preferred to stay with them rather than return to the man who was an enthusiastic supporter of the King's enemies. That political differences were largely the cause of the breakdown of the marriage can be deduced from Milton's explanation of how he came to write the divorce pamphlets:

> On this point, therefore, I published some books, and at that particular time, when man and wife were often the fiercest enemies, he being at home with his children, while she, the mother of the family, was in the camp of the enemy, threatening slaughter and destruction to her husband.

There is a similar passage in *Paradise Lost* (x. 899–908); but Aubrey expressed it more succinctly when he remarked of Milton's marriage that 'Two opinions doe not well on the same Boulster.'

Even without the Civil War the marriage was a misalliance. We need not suppose that Milton, as an opponent alleged, counted no woman a fit mate

> except she can speak Hebrew, Greek, Latin and French, and dispute against the Canon Law as well as you, or at least be able to hold discourse with you. But other Gentlemen of good quality are content with fewer and meaner endowments, as you know well enough.

But from the fact that Milton urges divorce for incompatibility rather than desertion it may be presumed that he found it less wounding to his pride to argue that he wished to leave his wife, and also that she had shown herself to be uninterested in the things that were nearest to his heart.

The shock of his wife's desertion was the first real disillusionment which Milton had suffered, and he wrote *The Doctrine and Discipline of Divorce* in an agony of spirit at finding he had blundered in his choice of a wife. The joy he had confidently expected was changed to bitterness.

He was a married man without a wife, a husband in-dissolubly bound to a woman he might never see again. But it is important to remember that although the occasion of the divorce pamphlets was determined by his personal circumstances, he did not suddenly acquire the views he expressed on the subject. His account in the *Second Defence* is substantially true:

> When the bishops, at whom every man aimed his arrow, had at length fallen, and we were now at leisure as far as they were concerned, I began to turn my thoughts to other subjects; to consider in what way I could contribute to the progress of real and substantial liberty, which is to be sought for not from without, but within, and is to be obtained prin-cipally not by fighting, but by the just regulation and by the proper conduct of life. Reflecting, therefore, that there are in all three species of liberty, without which it is scarcely possible to pass any life with comfort, namely, ecclesiastical, domestic or private, and civil: that I had already written on the first species and saw the magistrates diligently employed about the third, I undertook the domestic, which was the one that remained. But as this also appeared to be threefold, namely, whether the affair of marriage was rightly managed; whether the education of children was properly conducted; whether, lastly, we were to be allowed freedom of opinion, I explained my sentiments not only on the proper mode of contracting marriage, but also of dissolving it, should that be found necessary. . . . I next treated, in one little work, of the education of children. . . . Lastly, I wrote, after the model of a regular speech, *Areopagitica*, on the liberty of printing.

Of course it may be said that Milton wrote on divorce because his wife had deserted him, on freedom of speech because he could not expect to have his divorce pam-phlets licensed, and on education because he was a schoolmaster. These subjective reasons were doubtless present but we can tell from his Commonplace Book that he had liberal ideas about divorce some years before his marriage. The six pamphlets to which Milton refers, together with a revised edition of the first divorce pamphlet, all appeared in the space of two years.

Milton's main argument in the divorce pamphlets is that

> indisposition, unfitness, or contrariety of mind, arising from a cause in nature unchangeable, hindering, and ever likely to hinder the main benefits of conjugal society which are solace and peace

are greater reasons for divorce than the only two allowed in his time, impotence and adultery. 'This I amaze me at', he declares in *Tetrachordon*,

> that though all the superior and nobler ends both of marriage and of the married persons be absolutely frustrate, the matrimony stirs not, loses no hold, remains as rooted as the centre: but if the body bring but in a complaint of frigidity, by that cold application only this adamantine Alp of wedlock has leave to dissolve. . . . What courts of concupiscence are these, wherein fleshly appetite is heard before right reason, lust before love or devotion?

Marriage was designed by God to cure loneliness, but when the partners are badly matched the husband is brought to despair:

> The continual sight of his deluded thoughts without cure, must needs be to him, if especially his complexion incline him to melancholy, a daily trouble and pain of loss, in some degree like that which reprobates feel.

The chaste and virtuous man is more likely, by reason of his lack of experience, to be caught in the snare of indissoluble marriage:

> Who knowes not that the bashfull mutenes of a virgin may oft-times hide all the unlivelines and naturall sloth which is really unfit for conversation. . . . When as the sober man,

honouring the appearance of modesty . . . may easily chance
to meet, if not with a body inpenetrable, yet often with a
mind to all other due conversation inaccessible, and to all
the more estimable and superior purposes of matrimony use-
lesse and almost liveles.

In his profound disillusionment the man begins to hate,
from 'natural dissatisfaction and the turning aside from a
mistaken object'. He is tempted to fall into the sin of
despair:

> Though he be almost the strongest Christian, he will be
> ready to despair in vertue, and mutin against divine provi-
> dence: and this doubtles is the reason of those lapses and
> that melancholy despair which we see in many wedded per-
> sons, though they understand it not, or pretend other causes,
> because they know no remedy.

Many men are driven thereby to commit adultery, for
the soul

> wanders after that satisfaction which it had hope to find at
> home, but hath mist. Or els it sits repining even to Atheism;
> finding it self hardly dealt with, but misdeeming the cause to
> be in Gods Law, which is in mans unrighteous ignorance.

If he remains with his wife, he may 'grind in the mill of
an undelighted and servile copulation'. Far from being
one flesh, the married couple will 'be rather two car-
kasses chained unnaturally together; or, as it may happ'n,
a living soule bound to a dead corps.' Surely, Milton
argues, it is

> a lesse breach of wedlock to part with wise and quiet consent
> betimes, than still to soile and profane that mystery of joy
> and union with a polluting sadnes and perpetuall distemper;
> for it is not the outward continuing of mariage that keeps
> whole that cov'nant, but whosoever does most according to
> peace and love, whether in mariage, or in divorce, he it is
> that breaks mariage least.

Milton's conception of the true purpose of marriage is described in a beautiful passage in *Tetrachordon*:

We cannot therefore alwayes be contemplative, or pragmaticall abroad, but have need of som delightfull intermissions, wherin the enlarg'd soul may leav off a while her severe schooling; and like a glad youth in wandring vacancy, may keep her hollidaies to joy and harmless pastime: which as she cannot well do without company, so in no company so well as where the different sexe in most resembling unlikenes, and most unlike resemblance cannot but please best and be pleas'd in the aptitude of that variety. Wherof lest we should be too timorous, in the aw that our flat sages would form us and dresse us, wisest *Salomon* among his gravest Proverbs countenances a kinde of ravishment and erring fondnes in the entertainment of wedded leisures; and in the Song of Songs, which is generally beleev'd, even in the jolliest expressions to figure the spousals of the Church with Christ, sings of a thousand raptures betweene those two lovely ones farre on the hither side of carnall enjoyment. By these instances, and more which might be brought, we may imagine how indulgently God provided against mans loneliness; that he approv'd it not, as by himself declar'd not good; that he approv'd the remedy thereof, as of his own ordaining, consequently good; and as he ordain'd it, so doubtles proportionably to our fal'n estate he gives it; els were his ordinance at least in vain, and we for all his gifts still empty handed.

It is always the idealist who falls most heavily, and the difference between ideal and actual marriage in Milton's case left a permanent scar:

As no man apprehends what vice is, so well as he who is truly vertuous, no man knows hel like him who converses most in heav'n, so there is none that can estimate the evil and the affliction of a naturall hatred in matrimony, unlesse he have a soul gentle enough and spacious enough to contemplate what is true love.

For the sake of his sectarian audience, as well as for his own satisfaction, Milton was compelled to show that his views were supported by the Scriptures; and sometimes, especially in *Tetrachordon*, he forces the meaning of some of his quotations to suit his own purposes. He is on safer ground where he relies on first principles, as when he declares that

> God delights not to make a drudge of Virtue, whose actions must be all elective and unconstrained. Forc't Virtue is a Bolt overshot, it goes neither forward nor backward, and does no good as it stands.

In one famous sentence in *Tetrachordon* he even declares that 'no ordinance, human or from heaven, can bind against the good of man'. Milton, though unconsciously, was setting up his own convictions not only against the teaching of all the Churches, both Catholic and Protestant, but against the plain sense of the New Testament. Those who accept the sacramental view of marriage will reject Milton's conception of divorce. Others may complain that he does not consider the fate of the children, that easy divorce is apt to make marriage an unstable institution, and that he considers the question only from the man's point of view. Milton does admit that, though the man should normally be the master, there are cases where the wife is superior, and the 'wiser should govern the less wise, whether male or female'; but he believed that woman was created for man. He looked down on women and yet demanded of a wife qualities only to be found in an equal or superior; he wanted submissiveness and at the same time the companionship which depends on equality; he was intensely susceptible to feminine beauty, and yet believed that the passions should be governed by reason. But he may well have been right in believing that for civilized people incompatibility of

F

mind is more destructive of married happiness than adultery itself.

It has been suggested that the reception accorded to Milton's divorce pamphlets was a bigger shock to him even than his wife's desertion. Prynne spoke of Milton's views as *Divorce at Pleasure*, and called him

> a libertine, that thinketh his wife a Manacle, and his very garters to be shackles and fetters to him; one that (after the Independent fashion) will be tied to no obligation to God or man.

A preacher before parliament referred to the first divorce pamphlet as a wicked book which deserved to be burnt; and the Parliamentary Committee on licensing was ordered to interrogate the author. The Presbyterians, who before they acquired power had seemed to stand for freedom of speech and freedom of worship, showed that they were as represssive as the Bishops had been. Milton's feelings can be gauged from the difference in tone between the first divorce pamphlet and the last, entitled *Colasterion*, which was a reply to an anonymous attack. Professor Parker, indeed, remarks with some slight exaggeration that Milton's opponent was 'amazingly polite, and does little to deserve the storm of abuse in the *Colasterion*.' Milton was annoyed that his views on divorce had been answered, not by a worthy antagonist, but by someone who was unable even to understand his arguments. He therefore vented his anger on the anonymous nonentity, calling him 'an illiterate and arrogant presumer', a 'gross and sluggish, yet a contentious and overweening pretender', 'a drone', 'a phlegmy clod', a 'noisome fool', 'this most incogitant woodcock', 'a presumptuous lozel', 'this nuisance', 'this pork'. The pamphlet though amusing shows Milton at his worst, and it can be excused only as the utterance of a hurt and disillusioned man. But at the end of the pamphlet Milton promises to answer a serious criticism of his views in a totally different style.

In a sonnet written at this time Milton expressed his feelings on the detraction which followed upon his writing his divorce pamphlets:

> I did but prompt the age to quit their cloggs
>> By the known rules of antient libertie,
>> When strait a barbarous noise environs me
>> Of Owles and Cuckoes, Asses, Apes and Doggs.

From the literary point of view the most important result of the divorce controversy was that Milton was impelled to write his tract in defence of unlicensed printing, the most widely-read of his prose works. It has been estimated that before the new licensing law of June 1643 only one book in ten, if that, was published with a license. After the new law was passed, four books in every five were licensed, though *The Doctrine and Discipline of Divorce* was not. Milton wrote his *Areopagitica* because the unlearned and illiberal censors banned any work 'which contained views or sentiments at all above the level of vulgar superstition'. Milton wrote his pamphlet in the form of a speech addressed to Parliament, and he employed all the arts of rhetoric to persuade his readers. He aimed at convincing by reason; but the rational arguments are nevertheless subordinated to a burning sense of conviction which he hoped to persuade others to share.

Already in his first divorce pamphlet Milton had tried to show that 'Error supports Custom, Custom countenances Error'; that the 'Womb of Teeming Truth' is not closed up, though Truth when it is first propounded is invariably regarded as heretical:

Though this ill hap wait on her nativity, that she never comes

into the world, but like a Bastard, to the ignominy of him
that brought her forth;

and he had pointed to the pursuit of truth as a patriotic
duty: 'Let not England forget her precedence of teaching
nations how to live.' *Areopagitica* is really a development
of these ideas. Milton tried to show that licensing was
brought to perfection by the Inquisition; that the new
act would fail to suppress the very books at which it was
aimed; and that it was likely to hinder the search for
truth. Virtue and vice cannot be separated in literature
any more than they can in life.

Milton shows that once you start licensing new books
you may end by banning old ones. It would be difficult
to ban books of religious controversy, though they were
in fact the most dangerous. Then Milton shows that it
would be quite impracticable to license not only books,
but all kinds of amusements, and here his prose takes on a
tone of lofty irony:

If we think to regulat Printing, thereby to rectifie manners,
we must regulat all recreations and pastimes, all that is
delightfull to man. No musick must be heard, no song be
set or sung, but what is grave and *Dorick*. There must be
licencing dancers, that no gesture, motion, or deportment
be taught our youth but what by their allowance shall be
thought honest; for such *Plato* was provided of; It will
ask more than the work of twenty licencers to examin all
the lutes, the violins, and ghittarrs in every house; they
must not be suffer'd to prattle as they doe, but must
be licenc'd what they may say. And who shall silence
all the airs and madrigals, that whisper softnes in chambers? The Windows also, and the *Balcone's* must be
thought on, there are shrewd books, with dangerous
Frontispieces set to sale; who shall prohibit them, shall
twenty licensers? The villagers also must have their visitors
to enquire what lectures the bagpipe and the rebbeck reads
ev'n to the ballatry, and the gammuth of every municipal

fidler, for these are the Countrymans *Arcadia's* and his *Monte Mayors*. Next, what more Nationall corruption, for which England hears ill abroad, than houshold gluttony; who shall be the rectors of our daily riotting? and what shall be done to inhibit the multitudes that frequent those houses where drunk'nes is sold and harbour'd? Our garments also should be referr'd to the licensing of some more sober work-masters to see them cut into a lesse wanton garb.

Again and again Milton returns to the argument that you cannot make people virtuous by act of parliament since virtue depends on free will:

I cannot praise a fugitive and cloister'd vertue, unexercis'd & unbreath'd, that never sallies out and sees her adversary, but slinks out of the race, where that immortall garland is to be run for, not without dust and heat. Assuredly we bring not innocence into the world, we bring impurity much rather: that which purifies us is triall, and triall is by what is contrary. That vertue therefore which is but a youngling in the contemplation of evill, and knows not the utmost that vice promises to her followers, and rejects it, is but a blank vertue, not a pure; her whitenesse is but an excrementall whitenesse.

Although we can see from the satirical portrait of the Presbyterian who keeps his business and his religion in watertight compartments that Milton was disappointed with the parliamentary majority, he still exhorts parliament to rise to the height of their great opportunity of reforming the Reformation. London was the centre of the parliamentarian strength, and it was also a place of great intellectual ferment. 'Behold now this vast City', Milton exclaims,

a City of refuge, the mansion house of liberty, encompast and surrounded with his protection; the shop of warre hath not there more anvils and hammers waking, to fashion out the plates and instruments of armed Justice in defence of beleaguer'd Truth, than there be pens and heads there, sitting by their studious lamps, musing, searching, revolving new notions and ideas wherewith to present, as with their homage and their fealty the approaching Reformation: others as fast reading, trying all things, assenting to the force of reason and convincement.

England was 'a noble and puissant Nation rousing herself like a strong man after sleep, and shaking her invincible locks'. It can be seen from such a passage than in spite of the reception accorded to his divorce pamphlets, Milton still retained much of his earlier optimism. There were, of course, limits to his toleration. Writing when he did he could not be expected to extend it to Catholics or to Royalists. But in spite of these limitations *Areopagitica* remains the finest defence in our literature of freedom of speech, and it contains many memorable sentences on the necessity of liberty and on the value of literature:

> As good almost kill a Man as kill a good Book; who kills a Man kills a reasonable creature, Gods Image; but hee who destroyes a good Booke, kills reason it selfe, kills the Image of God, as it were in the eye. Many a man lives a burden to the Earth; but a good Booke is the pretious life-blood of a master spirit, imbalm'd and treasur'd up on purpose to a life beyond life.

Milton's plea fell on deaf ears, and there is some irony in the fact that during the Protectorate Milton himself became a censor though his main duty was to supervise the official journal of the Commonwealth, *Mercurius Politicus*. He was more like a supervisory editor than a licenser. One incident reveals the liberal spirit with which he carried out his distasteful task: when a printer was accused of publishing a Socinian catechism he declared that Milton had licensed it. Milton, on being interrogated, admitted the fact and pointed out that he had published a pamphlet in which he argued against the prohibition of books. In licensing this book, he said, he had done no more than follow his convictions.

He was referring, of course, not to his Socinian convictions, but to his belief in unlicensed printing.

In spite of his wifeless state, Milton seems to have led a sociable life. On the fall of Reading in April 1643 his father had come to live with him. The poet used to visit Captain Hobson, to whose wife he addressed the sonnet 'To the Lady Margaret Ley'. At about the same time he wrote another sonnet, probably to another lady

> that in the prime of earliest youth,
> Wisely hath shun'd the broad way and the green.

According to Edward Phillips, Milton had 'a design of marrying one of Dr. Davis's daughters, a very handsome and witty gentlewoman'. She was too wise, or too conventional, to ignore the existence of the first Mrs. Milton. Miss Davis is presumably the lady mentioned by Milton's other nephew—if he was the anonymous biographer—with whom the poet was in treaty for a marriage. Any such project was prevented by the unexpected return of Mary Milton. After the Battle of Naseby the Powells realized that the King's cause was lost, and they knew that Oxford, where they were living, could not hold out long. They therefore sent Mary to London. One evening when Milton was paying a customary visit to a relation, Mary, who had been waiting in another room, suddenly entered and begged pardon on her knees. At first, according to Edward Phillips, Milton made some show of aversion:

> but partly his own generous nature, more inclinable to Reconciliation than to perseverance in Anger and Revenge; and partly the strong intercession of Friends on both sides, soon brought him to an Act of Oblivion, and a firm League of Peace for the future.

Milton was about to move into a larger house, and Mary
lived with Christopher Milton's mother-in-law until the
move was completed. After the fall of Oxford, the
ruined Powells, including several brothers and sisters,
came to live with the Miltons, while Richard Powell was
trying to recover part of the possessions he had forfeited
by his royalist sympathies. It showed considerable mag-
nanimity on the poet's part to shelter this pack of his
wife's relations, even though he was anxious to recover
the old debt of £500 and Mary's £1,000 dowry. Powell
and Milton's father both died in 1647, but the rest of the
Powells stayed on for a while and we can tell from
Milton's letter to Carlo Dati that he found their presence
an intolerable burden:

> It is often a matter of sorrowful reflection to me that those
> with whom I have been linked by chance or the law, by pro-
> pinquity or some connection of no real meaning, are con-
> tinually at hand to infest my home, to stun me with their
> noise and wear out my temper, whilst those who are en-
> deared to me by the closest sympathy of tastes and pursuits
> are almost all denied me whether by death or by an insuper-
> able distance of place.

Mary, on her return, had pleaded that she had followed
her mother's advice; and we can tell from later proceed-
ings that Milton and Mrs. Powell disliked each other
heartily and that he clung to his legal rights with regard
to the unpaid dowry.

Mary's return marked the end of a chapter in Milton's
life; and the end of a literary chapter was marked by the
publication of his collected poems in January 1646.
With the defeat of the Royalists, the poets, unconsciously
submitting their *apologia* to posterity before the tempest
swept them away, collected their poems. Cowley's
Mistress, the 'late choice pieces' of Edmund Waller (mentioned in the preface to Milton's volume), Suckling's

posthumous *Fragmentea Aurea*, Herrick's *Hesperides*, and books by Cleveland, Stanley, Lovelace, Crashaw and Vaughan all appeared within the space of four years. Milton, too, felt the need of stocktaking. Since the completion of his education and apprenticeship by his visit to Italy seven years before, he had written only one Latin poem and a handful of sonnets. There was no prospect of writing his epic in the near future, if only because he had not made up his mind on his own theological position. So, for his collected poems, Milton chose another Virgilian epigraph, expressing apprehension lest the critic's evil tongue should harm the future poet—the poet of the unwritten epic. The book was fortified with the statement that 'the songs were set in Musick by Mr. Henry Lawes' and with the famous eulogy of *Comus* by Sir Henry Wotton. But though Milton offered his work to the public with some diffidence, as the earnest of future greatness rather than as the proof of fulfilment, he was unwilling to discard even his most trivial compositions. He printed paraphrases of the psalms which had astonished his family circle when he was still a schoolboy. He printed Latin verses, written as undergraduate exercises. He even included an unfinished poem on the Passion, an avowed failure. To many of the poems he attached dates, partly as an apology for their immaturity, but partly so that the reader could trace his poetical development. He omitted only two poems: the feeble lines on the death of his infant niece and 'At a Vacation Exercise'. These he characteristically preserved for publication in the second edition, nearly half a century after the date of composition. He preserved even the chips from his workshop, as though he realized that they would be of interest to posterity. Even the earliest poems, with the single exception of 'The Passion', are worthy to stand on their own merits. It was presumably included in the volume, in spite of its inferiority to the excluded poems, for the sake of its subject—Milton had fewer 'divine' poems than might have been expected by his Puritan friends. Few poets would emerge so triumphantly from the test of publishing everything they had written. If Milton had been hanged at the Restoration his reputation as a poet would depend almost entirely on this volume; but he would still be regarded as one of the three or four best English poets.

Chapter Five

POLITICS

DURING the next twelve years Milton was absorbed in politics, first as an apologist for the execution of Charles I, then as Secretary for Foreign Tongues under the Commonwealth and as official propagandist for the Puritan Revolution, and finally as an opponent of the Restoration. During this period he wrote very little verse, and even his prose works are less interesting as literature than his early pamphlets. He soon lost faith in the Presbyterians, partly because they had branded him as a heretic, but more because they had proved to be as intolerant to minority opinion as the Bishops had been and because they had hastened to enrich themselves. His bitterest attack on the Long Parliament occurs in a passage in his *History of Britain*, written probably soon after 1648. He laments that Parliament had failed to rise to its great opportunity. They had thrown away liberty. 'After many labours, much bloodshed, and vast expense' the hopes of good men had been brought to 'ridiculous frustration'. Everyone was out for his own profit.

> Then was justice delayed, and soon after denied; spight and favour determined all: hence faction, thence treachery, both at home and in the field: everywhere wrong and oppression: foul and dishonest things committed daily, or maintained, in secret, or in open.

Crooked politicians 'fell to huckster the commonwealth', and the people who had spent their blood or their property for the cause were cheated of their rights and 'tossed up and down after miserable attendance from one committee to another with petitions in their hands.'

The people, disappointed in their rulers, turned to lewdness or atheism, so that they made themselves unfit for liberty, 'for stories teach us, that liberty sought out of season, in a corrupt and degenerate age, brought Rome itself to a farther slavery.' Milton concluded that though Britain was a nation of warriors, 'it is naturally not over-fertile of men able to govern justly and prudently in peace.' If one compares this passage with Milton's patriotic confidence in his fellow-countrymen's wisdom only four years previously, one can gauge the extent of his disillusionment.

After Naseby, many of the vacant seats in the House of Commons had been filled by Independents, and Milton began to place his hopes on this minority. In a sonnet written at the time he upbraided the new forcers of conscience, the Presbyterians:

> Because you have thrown off your Prelate Lord,
>   And with stiff Vowes renounc'd his Liturgie
>   To seise the widdow'd whore Pluralitie
>   From them whose sin ye envi'd, not abhor'd,
> Dare ye for this adjure the Civill Sword
>   To force our Consciences that Christ set free?

The last line of the sonnet plays on the common derivation of the two words:

> *New Presbyter* is but *Old Priest* writ Large.

Between 1645 and 1649 Charles was a prisoner, first of the Scots and then of the army. The Levellers, the left-wing movement in the army, attacked the monarchy and the House of Lords, and demanded universal suffrage. Cromwell and Ireton, on the other hand, defended the rights of property and hoped that they would be able to come to terms with the King. The army debates at Putney in the summer and autumn of 1647, in which Cromwell and other leaders discussed political questions on equal terms with the rank and file, maintained a high level of argument, which bears witness to the intelligence and maturity of the soldiers. The Levellers thought the State should protect the welfare of the common people, but they were unrealistic in supposing that the shift of power they wanted could be brought about merely by devising a democratic constitution; Cromwell was anxious to make England safe for the men of property. When the Levellers became a serious danger to the propertied classes, he crushed them ruthlessly.

At the end of 1647 Charles made a secret treaty with the Scots, and two months later the second civil war broke out. Cromwell at last resolved 'to call Charles Stuart, that man of blood, to an account for that blood he had shed, and mischief he had done to his utmost, against the Lord's Cause and People in these poor Nations.' The English Presbyterians still wished to preserve the monarchy; but the army and the Independents believed that there could be no peace so long as the King was alive. After the surrender of Colchester and the defeat of the Scots at Preston, the Presbyterians, who were known to be hostile to the army, were excluded from Parliament by means of Pride's Purge. On 1 January, 1649, the Rump agreed to bring the King to trial, and four weeks later he was duly executed.

Meanwhile, when Fairfax was besieging Colchester, Milton had exhorted him to clean up the State as soon as victory had been achieved:

> O yet a nobler task awaites thy hand;
> For what can Warr, but endless warr still breed,
> Till Truth, & Right from Violence be freed,
> And Public Faith cleard from the shamefull brand

> Of Public Fraud. In vain doth Valour bleed
> While Avarice, & Rapine share the land.

It is not surprising, therefore, that Milton should approve of Pride's Purge. The second civil war convinced him that the King was not to be trusted, and as soon as he knew that the trial was to take place he began to write *The Tenure of Kings and Magistrates*, partly to justify the trial and execution, and partly to attack the Presbyterians for their desertion. Milton purports to prove

> that it is lawful, and hath been held so through all ages, for any, who hath the power, to call to account a tyrant, or wicked king, and after due conviction, to depose and put him to death; if the ordinary magistrates have neglected, or denied to do it.

Since the Rump represented the army rather than the nation as a whole Milton could not really claim that the execution of the King was the will of the people. This did not unduly perturb him since he believed that it was the duty of the wise and good to rule the rest. He believed in liberty, but not in equality. In other respects he came close to the democratic opinions of the Levellers. He condemned the theory that Kings were accountable to God alone, and he claimed that their power was derived from the people: even if the trial of the King was without precedent, it was all the more courageous for that and it might serve as a precedent for future ages.

The Tenure was written in a few weeks so that it could be published almost at the time of the execution of the King, and it naturally lacks the grandeur of Milton's best prose. He is most effective in his attacks on the wretched Presbyterians who had fought against the King, and who were therefore guilty of rebellion in spite of their change of front.

A month after the publication of the pamphlet Milton's efforts were rewarded by his appointment as Secretary for Foreign Tongues. His job was to translate into Latin despatches to foreign governments, and to translate foreign despatches into English; but he was also expected from time to time to write propaganda on behalf of the commonwealth. Milton accepted the post, though he knew that it would mean a further postponement of his epic. His first task was to write a reply to the *Eikon Basilike*, a book of meditations allegedly written by King Charles during his imprisonment, though actually composed by his chaplain. This dull little book went through forty-six editions in twelve months and aroused much sympathy for the royal martyr. Milton disliked the task and he afterwards claimed that he

> did not insult over fallen majesty, as is pretended; I only preferred Queen Truth to King Charles. The charge of insult, which I foresaw the malevolent would urge, I was at some pains to remove in the beginning of the work; and as often as possible in other places. (F)

On the whole Milton's claim is justified. Though *Eikonoklastes* is one of the dullest of Milton's works, refuting his opponent paragraph by paragraph, his invective is generally restrained and objective, at least to those who are not Royalist. His attacks on the ignorance of the established clergy are too sweeping, and some of his accusations against Charles show a lamentable willingness to believe the worst. But there is one passage which has done a great deal of harm to Milton's reputation. He discovered that one of the prayers attributed to the King was taken from Sidney's *Arcadia*, so he absurdly accused Charles of being an irreligious and hypocritical thief because he stole the prayer from Sidney's 'vain amatorious poem' which, though full of worth and wit, was not worthy to be named 'among religious thoughts and duties.' He derided the Royalists for not having recognized this 'ethnic prayer'; and he jeered at the Bishops because the King borrowed from Sidney rather than from 'the rheum of their mellifluous prayers and meditations'. Milton was adopting the Calvinist view that 'however rich the Scriptures and Christian tradition may be in recorded prayers, all prayer should be simply an ever-renewed effort to re-embody the petitions of the Lord's Prayer'.[1] The use of Sidney's prayer was unimportant beside the forgery of the whole *Eikon Basilike*, and the prayer was better from most points of view than the extempore prayers beloved of the Puritans; but however much we may condemn Milton for this passage, there is no reason to believe, as some have argued, that Milton himself inserted the prayer in a specially printed edition of the *Eikon Basilike* so that he could jeer at it.

A month after the publication of *Eikonoklastes* a professor at Leyden of international reputation, Claude de Saumaise (Salmasius) attacked the English people in his *Defensio Regia*. Milton was instructed by the Council to write a reply. There was a good reason why he should have asked to be excused. He had already lost the sight of one eye and he had been warned by his physicians that the new labour would involve the loss of the other. He tells us that he 'would not have listened to the voice even of Aesculapius himself in preference to the suggestions of the heavenly monitor within [his] breast'. But although his conscience—or his super-ego—made him accept the task without hesitation, he wrote under appalling handicaps, compelled, as he tells us, 'to break off almost every hour'. Under the circumstances it was a remarkable feat to accomplish the work—written, of course, in the international language, Latin—in under

---

[1] Merrit Y. Hughes, *The Review of English Studies*, 1952, p. 140. This article contains the best discussion of the alleged forgery.

twelve months. *The Defence of the English People* was a resounding success and Salmasius was crushed. He lost his credit with Queen Christina of Sweden, as Milton afterwards boasted, and his reply remained unpublished for several years. Milton became internationally famous or notorious: and distinguished visitors to England made a point of calling on him.

The book suffers from the defects of most propaganda. Salmasius is ridiculed for his miserable bald Latin, his puerility, and his tittle-tattle; he is stigmatized as a vain and flashy man, a worm, a very brute, a cuckoo and a Judas. But although Milton indulges in the small change of invective, he does answer his adversary's arguments one by one, and if the book is now unread and almost unreadable, it is because it is linked too closely to Salmasius's. Milton's main argument is sensible enough: that in a Christian country the king should be the people's servant; that 'whatever things are for the universal good of the whole state, are for that reason lawful and just'; that 'no man by the law of nature has the right to be king, unless he excel all others in wisdom and courage'; that Parliament, or the people 'are superior to kings, be they good or bad'; and that kings are subject to the law. Milton is illogical when he tries to argue that Charles had been executed according to the will of the people, 'for whatever the better and sounder part of parliament did, in which the true Power of the people resides, why may not the people be said to have done it?' The case for the execution of Charles I could not rest on the general will.

The physicians were right in their prophecy, though the exact cause of Milton's blindness is still a matter of debate. It has been diagnosed as amaurosis and glaucoma, brought on by eye-strain over a long period of years, and perhaps connected with gout. Milton bore

G

his misfortune with fortitude and religious resignation. He was upheld by the thought that he had lost his eyes in a noble cause. As he told Cyriack Skinner:

> The conscience, Friend, to have lost them overply'd
> In libertyes defence, my noble task,
> Of which all Europe talks from side to side.
> This thought might lead me through the world's vain mask
> Content though blind, had I no better guide.

But we can see that he achieved resignation only after a severe struggle. The lamentations of Samson and the invocation to Light in the Third Book of *Paradise Lost* are the public fruits of that struggle; in the more personal sonnet Milton characteristically uses his blindness as the occasion for a renewed dedication of his talents to God:

> When I consider how my light is spent,
> E're half my days, in this dark world and wide,
> And that one Talent which is death to hide,
> Lodg'd with me useless, though my Soul more bent
> To serve therewith my Maker, and present
> My true account, least he returning chide,
> Doth God exact day-labour, light deny'd
> I fondly ask; But patience to prevent
> That murmur, soon replies, God doth not need
> Either man's work or his own gifts, who best
> Bear his milde yoak, they serve him best, his State
> Is Kingly. Thousands at his bidding speed
> And post o're Land and Ocean without rest:
> They also serve who only stand and waite.

To the Royalists, even to the poet Bishop King, Milton had been stricken blind for attacking the memory of Charles the Martyr. To such an attack Milton made a dignified reply in his *Second Defence of the English People*:

Let the calumniators of God's judgments cease to revile me, and to forge their superstitious dreams about me. Let them be assured that I neither regret my lot nor am ashamed of it, that I remain unmoved and fixed in my opinion, that I neither believe nor feel myself an object of God's anger, but actually experience and acknowledge His fatherly mercy and kindness to me in all matters of greatest moment—especially in that I am able, through his consolation and his strengthening of my spirit, to acquiesce in his divine will, thinking oftener of what he has bestowed upon me than of what he has withheld. . . . If the choice were necessary, I would, sir, prefer my blindness to yours; yours is a cloud spread over the mind, which darkens both the light of reason and conscience; mine keeps from my view only the coloured surfaces of things, while it leaves me at liberty to contemplate the beauty and stability of virtue and truth. (F)

He was more perturbed by the accusation that he was ugly, lean, bloodless, and shrivelled, and he was careful to state both here and in the sonnet to Skinner that his eyes are clear

> To outward view, of blemish or of spot.

Milton had been ordered to answer the anonymous reply to his *First Defence* entitled *Regii Sanguinis Clamor* (*The Royal Blood crying to Heaven*). This had been written by Peter du Moulin and it was published with an unsigned preface by Alexander More. Hearing that Milton was planning a reply, More in some agitation denied the authorship. He was at least an accomplice, and Milton did not wish to waste the invective he had so diligently prepared. Years later, after the Restoration, du Moulin congratulated himself on having escaped certain destruction at Milton's hands by preserving his anonymity. His attack on the poet is violent and scurrilous, and Milton might have wished to reply to it, even without the Council's instructions. But in 1652 he was feeling low in health and spirits. He had had to make the difficult adjustment to his blindness during the previous year, and he probably never saw his only son, John, born in March 1651. The third of his three daughters, Deborah, was born on 2 May, 1652. The infant survived, but the mother died three days afterwards, and the boy died about the middle of June. Stunned by this double blow, Milton found it difficult to settle down to political polemics. Perhaps it was his temporary feeling of Heaven's desertion, which was later to find expression in *Samson Agonistes*, that led him in August 1653 to put the first eight psalms into flat and feeble verse. He could comfort himself with the thoughts of the psalmist. He had not walked astray in counsel of the wicked; his foes had said 'No help for him in God there lies'; and he could pray that God would destroy those 'that speak a lie'.

It is usually assumed that Milton's relations with his wife between the date of her return and her death were not particularly happy, and Mary has been regarded as the model for Dalila. It is true that on the evidence of the divorce pamphlets we should not expect them to have many interests in common, and Mary was presumably distressed by the legal bickering with the Powell family. But the troubles Milton was to have with his daughters cannot be taken as proof that they sided with their mother, for the eldest was only five at the time of Mary's death. According to Milton's nephews, who must have known the truth even if they did not tell it, Mary lived in good accord with her husband until her death. If we could accept Professor W. R. Parker's theory, Milton commemorated not his second wife but his first in one of the most beautiful of his sonnets. She like the late espoused Saint of the sonnet died as the result of child-birth: Katharine Milton, we are told, died of consumption, though this may have been brought on by the birth of a child four months previously. It is implied in line 7 that Milton had seen his wife in reality, and though he may have been acquainted with Katharine for some years, he did not marry her until after he became blind.

> Methought I saw my late espoused Saint
>   Brought to me like *Alcestis* from the grave,
>   Whom *Joves* great Son to her glad Husband gave,
>   Rescu'd from death by force though pale and faint,
> Mine as who washt from spot of child-bed taint,
>   Purification in the old Law did save,
>   And such, as yet once more I trust to have
>   Full sight of her in Heaven without restraint,
> Came vested all in white, pure as her mind:
>   Her face was vail'd, yet to my fancied sight,
>   Love, sweetness, goodness, in her person shin'd
> So clear, as in no face with more delight.
>   But O as to embrace me she enclin'd
>   I wak'd, she fled, and day brought back my night.

Three other sonnets belong to the same period of Milton's life. The one addressed to Sir Henry Vane compliments him on his wisdom in knowing what severed spiritual from civil power; the others, in the Horatian mode, are invitations to dinner, and they show that Milton had remarkable powers of recuperation. He invites his pupil Lawrence to a 'neat repast' with wine and music, and in the similar sonnet addressed to Skinner, another pupil, he reproves the Puritan who objects to any form of relaxation:

> That with superfluous burden loads the day,
> And when God sends a cheerful hour, refrains.

The *Second Defence* was at last published in May 1654. By this time Cromwell had dismissed the Rump, and its successor, the Barebones Parliament, which consisted of unpractical idealists, dissolved itself in December 1653, handing over its power to Cromwell, who became Lord Protector. Milton began by approving of the Barebones Parliament, but he was soon disgusted with its ineffectiveness and he had no tears for its dissolution.

> They meet, but do nothing; and having wearied themselves by their mutual dissensions, and fully exposed their incapacity to the observation of the country, they consent to a voluntary dissolution.

Milton praised Cromwell as the protector of England's liberties, one who deserved to rule because he was without selfish ambition; and although a dictatorship was not an ideal form of government, he thought that the people were not yet ready to govern themselves. His panegyric of the Lord Protector was enthusiastic, but it was far from servile. He warns Cromwell not to entrench on the liberties of others; he urges him to make use of the services of his former comrades-in-arms; and he lays down a programme of reform—the abolition of a State Church, the establishment of toleration, the minimum of legislation, better provision for education, and the abolition of the censorship. Inevitably Cromwell proved to be a disappointment. He strengthened the established Church; he sacked the men Milton most admired, Vane, Bradshaw and Overton; he conferred knighthoods; and above all he tried to force citizens to be virtuous. It is not surprising, therefore, that after Cromwell's death Milton's pamphlets are full of denunciations of dictatorship. But when he wrote the *Second Defence* Milton's eulogy of Cromwell was perfectly sincere, and his portraits of Cromwell and the other Commonwealth leaders form the most interesting part of the book, with the exception of the long autobiographical passage in which he replies to his traducers.

Before the war he had meditated an epic which would celebrate England as Camoens had celebrated Portugal. Now Milton had lived through one of the great events in English history, and there is no doubt that he regarded his two *Defences* as a kind of substitute for the unwritten epic. He claims that his subject 'was never surpassed in any age, in dignity or in interest'. He imagines that Europe is waiting on his words:

> I seem to survey, as from a towering height, the far extended tracts of sea and land, and innumerable crowds of spectators, betraying in their looks the liveliest interest and sympathy.

At the end of the *Second Defence* he deliberately compares himself to an epic poet:

> I have delivered my testimony, I would almost say, have erected a monument, that will not readily be destroyed, to the reality of those singular and mighty achievements which were above all praise. As the epic poet, who adheres at all to the rules of that species of composition, does not profess to describe the whole life of the hero whom he celebrates, but only some particular action of his life . . . so it will be sufficient, either for my justification or apology, that I have heroically celebrated at least one exploit of my countrymen; I pass by the rest, for who could recite the achievements of a whole people? (F)

He goes on to say that even if people are wanting to complete the political task, at least

> they were not wanting who could rightly counsel, exhort, inspire, and bind an unfading wreath of praise round the brows of the illustrious actors in so glorious a scene.

But the wreath has sadly faded, and the *Defences* are read only because they were written by the author of *Paradise Lost*.

A large part of the *Second Defence* is devoted to a racy and even Rabelaisian attack on More's sexual morals.

Milton is a master of contemptuous indignation and these
sections need to be translated by a Nashe rather than into
the more decorous English of the eighteenth century.

One passage in the *Second Defence* is of great importance
for our understanding of Milton's views on Christian
liberty. It occurs near the end in an exhortation to his
fellow-countrymen to show in time of peace qualities
comparable to those they had displayed in war.

> War has made many great whom peace makes small. If after
> being released from the toils of war, you neglect the arts of
> peace, if your peace and your liberty be a state of warfare,
> if war be your only virtue, the summit of your praise, you
> will, believe me, soon find peace the most adverse to your
> interests. Your peace will be only a more distressing war;
> and that which you imagined liberty will prove the worst of
> slavery. . . . Then, as if God was weary of protecting you,
> you will be seen to have passed through the fire that you
> might perish in the smoke. (F)

Milton had come to realize, as Coleridge was later to
do, that

> The sensual and the dark rebel in vain,
> Slaves to their own compulsion.

To possess freedom you have to deserve it; and Milton
tells the undeservers:

> Know that to be free is the same thing as to be pious, wise,
> temperate, just, frugal, abstinent, magnanimous, and brave;
> so to be the opposite of all these is to be a slave. . . . If
> you think slavery an intolerable evil, learn obedience to
> reason and the government of yourselves, and bid adieu to
> your dissensions, your jealousies, your superstitions, and
> your lusts.

Milton required not merely a government but a whole
population of virtuous men, but the politician has to do
with erring and sinful men, including himself. The gulf

between the ideal and reality was one of the reasons which led Milton finally to decide to write on the Fall of Man.

Although the *Second Defence* is more interesting to us, because of its autobiographical passages, than the *First Defence*, it made much less stir and had a comparatively small sale. It was not Milton's last contribution to the controversy. In the following year he wrote a *Defence of Himself* against More's charge that when he wrote the *Second Defence* he knew perfectly well that More was not the author of the book to which it was a reply. Milton's answer on this point is hardly convincing.

As part of his official duties Milton in 1655 wrote a letter of protest to the Duke of Savoy on the massacre of the Vaudois Protestants, and his private feelings on the question overflowed into one of the finest of his sonnets. His blindness necessitated the appointment of an assistant in his work. His salary was reduced to a pension, but he continued, in a subordinate capacity, to write letters down to the eve of the Restoration. In 1657, five years after his first application for the post, Andrew Marvell became Milton's colleague, and the admiration of the younger poet was warmly reciprocated by Milton. He was one of the very few men living at the time who was capable of appreciating Milton's poetry without being repelled by his political opinions.

Meanwhile Milton had married again, a fatherless girl of twenty-eight years of age named Katharine Woodcock, who lived with her mother in the suburb of Hackney. The marriage took place in November 1656. Eleven months later a daughter was born; but Katharine Milton died of consumption in February 1658, and the baby soon followed her to the grave. In spite of his bereavement Milton began the composition of his epic and he worked during the autumn and winter of each year; in the spring and summer his inspiration dried up. But *Paradise Lost* was not Milton's only literary work during the last few years of the Commonwealth. He appears to have worked on his treatise on *Christian Doctrine*, besides continuing his *History of Britain* and a Latin Thesaurus. He brought out a second edition of the *First Defence* with a preface in which he alludes to the epic which would be an even greater work; and on the eve of the Restoration he wrote another group of pamphlets.

In *A Treatise of Civil Power in Ecclesiastical Causes*, dedicated to the restored Rump, Milton tried to show that 'it is not lawful for any power on earth to compel in matters of religion'. Since Protestants believe that the interpretation of the Scriptures depends on the conscience of the individual, Milton argues that neither church nor magistrate has the right to be the final arbiter, and that men should no longer suffer in matters of religion 'that law of terror and satisfaction belonging now only to civil crimes'. A few months later Milton followed up this pamphlet with an attack on a State Church. *The Likeliest Means to Remove Hirelings Out of the Church* was by the abolition of tithes and salaries.

As the Restoration approached Milton produced pamphlet after pamphlet in a vain effort to avert the inevitable. Most of these are short and of little permanent interest. But *The Ready and Easy Way to Establish A Free Commonwealth*, the second edition of which appeared only a month before Charles II returned to his kingdom, is a courageous, if futile, plea for the good old cause. Milton, realizing the 'general defection of a misguided and abused Multitude' and the certainty that a popular vote would lead to the restoration of the monarchy, proposes a very limited suffrage. He thinks it intolerable that the many who are willing to give up their freedom should enslave the few who value it; and he argued that the minority should compel the majority to retain their liberty. Democracies, as we have cause to know, have sometimes voted away their freedom. Milton therefore proposes to have a senate elected by a restricted suffrage, one-third of the senate to come up for re-election every two or three years. To mitigate the oligarchic flavour of this proposal, he proposes that each county should have a local assembly, democratically elected. These assemblies would make their own laws, and appoint their own judges; and they would even have the power of rejecting or confirming the laws passed by the senate. Milton hoped that this decentralization would

> soon spread much more knowledge and Civility, yea, Religion, through all parts of the Land, by communicating the natural heat of Government and Culture more distributively to all extreme parts, which now lie numb and neglected.

Milton despised the fickleness of the mob; but he realized that what the people needed to make them responsible citizens was a liberal and religious education. Although he believed in a governing class, whose claims to rule depended not on birth or wealth but on spiritual insight,[1] the liberties for which he fought during the two decades which ended with the Restoration are necessary adjuncts to a properly functioning democracy—freedom of speech, freedom of worship, toleration, separation of Church and State, reasonable divorce laws, a generous educational programme, official encouragement of science and the arts, and the abolition of improper privilege. The great republican had an impressive political programme, but the English people preferred the prospect of a good time to the more austere delights of a Christian society—especially as the Puritans had displayed

[1] Their possession of this insight was shown by their holding of Miltonic views.

the rigours but not the graces of the ideal society en-
visaged by their greatest spokesman. Apart from that, as
Milton's friend, the author of *Oceana*, shrewdly observed, the Puritan revolution was doomed to failure if
only because they had not dispossessed the Royalists of
their estates.

Chapter Six

PROSE AND SONNETS

IF Milton had never written a line of verse he would still be numbered among the great English writers. Yet his prose has often been adversely criticized. It is complained that his style is modelled on that of Cicero and that it is un-English in structure and vocabulary; that his sentences are so long that the reader loses his way before he reaches the end; that he is apt to be turgid and humourless; and that his pages are disfigured by passages of scurrilous invective and heavy sarcasm. But it is impossible to dispose of Milton as a prose stylist by generalizations of this kind, if only because he had not one style but several. In the last pamphlet of all, *Of True Religion*, and even in the group of pamphlets written just before the Restoration, the style is by no means Ciceronian in structure or latinized in vocabulary. Milton writes in short sentences, good, strong, honest, plain sentences, hard-hitting and colloquial: they are totally different from those of the first four pamphlets. In his last period Milton wrote a prose as plain and direct as that demanded by the anti-imaginative members of the Royal Society: there are no 'lushious metaphors', no elaborate rhetorical artifice, no obscurity, and the style is far less ornate than that of Marvell's prose satires. Then again, the prose of the *History of Britain* is quite different from that of the divorce pamphlets, and the narrative parts of the *History* differ in turn from the long digression in which Milton discusses the failure of the revolution.

99

These differences are largely due to the thirty years
that had elapsed between the first pamphlet and the last:
the taste had in the interval radically changed. This was
partly caused by the influence of French models on the
exiled Royalists, and partly by the conscious search for
greater scientific precision under the influence of the
Royal Society. In the second half of the century there
was a strong reaction against the ornate prose of such
writers as Donne, Jeremy Taylor and Sir Thomas
Browne: but this reaction was assisted (as Mr. Harold
Fisch has reminded us) by the Puritan distrust of literary
sermons, and their deliberate search for simplicity of
expression. More important still, the period between
1640 and 1660 was an era of pamphleteering, and the
necessity of writing quickly before the situation changed,
and of appealing to as wide an audience as possible,
naturally affected the kind of prose in which pamphlets
were written. Milton wrote in several different styles,
mainly because he was addressing several different pub-
lics. His early pamphlets on episcopacy were addressed
to a comparatively learned audience, his divorce
pamphlets and *Areopagitica* primarily to Members of Parliament and other well-educated people, and his last
pamphlets to anyone who was able to read. He was discussing in them not church discipline or divorce law (on
which, indeed, he afterwards regretted he had not written in Latin) but immediate political issues. The early
pamphlets had been written to persuade the leaders of
opinion; the later ones appealed over the heads of the
leaders to the ordinary citizens. It may be, too, that
Milton simplified his style because the later pamphlets
had to be dictated, though it must be admitted that
Henry James used a more complicated style after he
began to dictate his novels.

There is some truth in the suggestion that Milton

learnt how to write English by an apprenticeship in the writing of Latin prose—not merely at school, but in the prolusions he composed at Cambridge. Masson thought that the last of these was one of the finest pieces of Latin prose ever written by an Englishman. As Dr. Tillyard says: 'It is a superb piece of writing. The Latin has disengaged itself from the trammels of academic rhetoric, and rises and falls with the ease and sweep of accomplished eloquence.' Here for example is a passage in which Milton describes how knowledge enables man to have dominion over nature:

> Sic tandem, Auditores, cum omnimoda semel eruditio suos orbes confecerit, non contentus iste spiritus tenebricoso hoc ergastulo eousque late aget se, donec et ipsum mundum, et ultra longe divina quadam magnitudine expatiata compleverit. Tum demum plerique casus atque eventus rerum ita subito emergent, ut ei, qui hanc arcem sapientiae adeptus est, nihil pene incautum, nihil fortuitum in vita possit accidere; videbitur sane is esse, cujus imperio et dominationi astra obtemperent, terra et mare obsecundent, venti tempestatesque morigerae sint; cui denique ipsa Parens Natura in deditionem se tradiderit, plane ac si quis Deus abdicato mundi imperio, huic jus ejus, et leges, administrationemque tanquam praefectori cuidam commisisset.

Milton's later Latin prose style was praised by Andrew Marvell after he had received a copy of one of the Defences. He told Milton:

> I shall now studie it even to the getting of it by Heart: esteeming it according to my poor Judgement (which yet I wish it were so right in all Things else) as the most compendious Scale, for so much, to the Height of the Roman Eloquence. When I consider how equally it turns and rises with so many figures, it seems to me a Trajans Columne in whose winding Ascent we see imboss'd the severall Monuments of your learned Victoryes.

Milton seems to have given some thought to the importance of prose style two or three years before he intervened in the episcopacy controversy. He told an Italian friend that 'when the language falls into corruption and decay' the downfall of the State is imminent. Debasement of a language is accompanied by 'a proneness to submit to any form of slavery'. Nearly twenty years later, after most of his own prose had been written, he outlined to Henri de Bras the qualities necessary for the historian. Just as he believed that the poet should lead a life that was a true poem, so he thought that the historian should be as noble as the hero of his story. Dignity, impressiveness and purity of style depended on the character of the writer. He declares that he does not demand an ornate style, and he sets Sallust above Tacitus. It is significant that this condemnation of the ornate was written after his own style had been simplified. But Milton believed that the style should vary according to the kind of work in which it was used. A rhetorical appeal, such as *Areopagitica*, properly demanded a more orotund style than the sober narration of events characteristic of the *History*, though when he draws the contemporary parallel he allows himself a sweep and sonority he had elsewhere eschewed. Yet all these different styles are Miltonic: they are the man himself in his integrity, his single-mindedness, and his pride. In the *Apology for Smectymnuus* Milton tells us that true eloquence depends on a passionate love of truth:

> For me, readers although I cannot say that I am utterly untrained in those rules which best rhetoricians have given, or unacquainted with those examples which the prime authors of eloquence have written in any learned tongue, yet true eloquence I find to be none but the serious and hearty love of truth: and that those whose mind soever is fully possessed with a fervent desire to know good things, and

with the dearest charity to infuse the knowledge of them into others, when such a man would speak, his words (by what I can express) like so many nimble and airy servitors trip about him at command, and in well-ordered files, as he would wish, fall aptly into their own places.

In one of the pamphlets on episcopacy Milton defends his use of vehement expressions on the grounds that he is concerned with truth:

And herewithal I invoke the Immortal Deity, Revealer and Judge of Secrets, That wherever I have in the Book plainly and roundly (though worthily and truly) . . . inveighed against Error and Superstition with vehement expressions: I have done it, neither out of malice, nor list to speak evil, nor any vain glory: but out of mere necessity, to vindicate the spotless Truth from an ignominious bondage.

In the same pamphlet he wrote:

The very essence of Truth is plainness, and brightness: the darkness and crookedness is our own. The Wisdom of God created understanding, fit and proportionable to Truth the object, and end of it, as the eye to the thing visible. If our understanding have a film of ignorance over it, or be blear with gazing on other false glisterings, what is that to Truth?

Although some readers may feel that Milton was often mistaken in his opinions and tragically cocksure in his certainty that he was always right, there is no reason to doubt that he always wrote what he believed to be the truth.

It is impossible to arrive at a true appreciation of Milton as a writer of prose unless we realize that the arts of rhetoric, which he had studied in Greek and Latin models, in Bacon, Hooker and Ralegh, were all subordinated in his own mind to a fervent desire to persuade others of truths which he had reached himself by the use

H

of right reason. But from the literary point of view, it must be confessed, his later prose is less interesting than his earlier. His last pamphlet approximates in style to that of countless lesser writers. The pamphlets on episcopacy, divorce, and the freedom of the press are more distinctively Miltonic, and they possess a grandeur which can hardly be matched outside the seventeenth century, and which is worthy to stand beside the best prose of Donne and Taylor. As an example of the early prose we may instance the prayer with which *Of Reformation* concludes, superb in its sustained rhythms, the organization of its sonorous clauses, and its slow building up to a climax, or the passage already quoted from *Animadversions upon the Remonstrant's Defence*.

As an example of the second period of Milton's prose we may refer to the passages already quoted in Chapter 4 from the divorce pamphlets and *Areopagitica*. But one further passage may be quoted from the latter, which proves that on occasion Milton could be witty. It describes the business man who puts religion and business in watertight compartments:

A man may be a heretick in the truth; and if he beleeve things only because his Pastor sayes so, or the Assembly so determins, without knowing other reason, though his belief be true, yet the very truth he holds, becomes his heresie. There is not any burden that som would gladlier post off to another, than the charge and care of their Religion. There be, who knows not that there be of Protestants and professors who live and dye in as arrant an implicit faith, as any lay Papist of Loretto. A wealthy man addicted to his pleasure and to his profits, finds Religion to be a traffick so entangl'd, and of so many piddling accounts, that of all mysteries he cannot skill to keep a stock going upon that trade. What should he doe? fain he would have the name to be religious, fain he would bear up with his neighbours in that. What does he therefore, but resolvs to give over toyling, and to find himself out som factor, to whose care and credit he may commit the whole managing of his religious affairs; som Divine of note and estimation that must be. To him he adheres, resigns the whole ware-house of his religion, with all the locks and keyes into his custody; and indeed makes the very person of that man his religion; esteems his associating with him a sufficient evidence and commendatory of his own piety. So that a man may say his religion is now no more within himself, but is becom a dividuall movable, and goes and comes neer him, according as that good man frequents the house. He entertains him, gives him gifts, feasts him, lodges him; his religion comes hom at night, praies, is liberally supt, and sumptuously laid to sleep, rises, is saluted, and after the malmsey, or some well spic't bruage, and better breakfasted than he whose morning appetite would have gladly fed on green figs between *Bethany* and *Ierusalem*, his Religion walks abroad at eight, and leavs his kind entertainer in the shop trading all day without his religion.

It can be seen from this passage that Milton was able, when he wished, to write plain and straightforward prose. He is no longer preaching or delivering an oration; the diction is not unduly latinized; and the sentence-structure is in accord with the genius of the language. The same thing may be said of the divorce pamphlets; and in the pamphlets written on the eve of the Restoration, Milton adopted an even more colloquial style. The following is a passage from *A Ready and Easy Way to Establish a free Commonwealth*, in which Milton discusses the disadvantages of monarchy:

Nay, it is well and happy for the People if their King be but a Cipher, being oft times a Mischief, a Pest, a scourge of the Nation, and which is worse, not to be removed, not to be controlled, much less accused or brought to punishment, without the danger of a common ruin, without the shaking and almost subversion of the whole Land: whereas in a free

Commonwealth, any Governor or chief Counsellor offending, may be removed and punished without the least Commotion. Certainly then that People must needs be mad or strangely infatuated, that build the chief hope of their common happiness or safety on a single Person; who if he happen to be good, can do no more than another man; if to be bad, hath in his hands to do more evil without check, than millions of other men. The happiness of a Nation must needs be firmest and certainest in a full and free Council of their own electing, where no single Person, but Reason only sways. And what madness is it for them who might manage nobly their own Affairs themselves, sluggishly and weakly to devolve all on a single Person: and more like Boys under Age than Men, to commit all to his patronage and disposal, who neither can perform what he undertakes, and yet for undertaking it, though royally paid, will not be their Servant, but their Lord? How unmanly must it needs be, to count such a one the breath of our Nostrils, to hang all our felicity on him, all our safety, our well-being, for which if we were aught else but Sluggards or Babies, we need depend on none but God and our own Counsels, our own active Virtue and Industry.

This is admirable in its way, but in the pamphlets on episcopacy, divorce, and freedom of the press, Milton displays an extraordinary energy which is apparent in the gusto of the tumultuous periods, in the uninhibited torrent of invective, in the enormous vocabulary and linguistic daring, and in the flash of illumination that comes from imaginative imagery. We get the impression of a mind, conscious of its powers, working at fever-heat, and able to shape to artistic purposes the learning and even the pedantry which would have stultified a lesser writer.

Milton's prose was not generally admired by his contemporaries; from the standpoint of the new age, Milton's prose was too eloquent, too eccentric, too far from colloquial speech. His very merits as a prose-writer and his ability to look beyond the immediate political issues may well have limited the contemporary effectiveness of his pamphlets. Hardly anyone took his advice. As a political writer he was for the most part a voice crying in the wilderness, and even *Areopagitica*, as far as we know, made only one contemporary convert. His real political influence was posthumous—with the Whigs of 1688 and the Americans of the eighteenth century.

Milton's sonnets were written half a century after the great Elizabethan sequences, and all the best-known poets of his age avoided the form, presumably because they felt that its possibilities had been exhausted. Milton, after his first efforts, five of which were in Italian, eschewed the theme of love, and he adopted the Italian form, though in some of his best sonnets he avoids a break between octave and sestet. Of the ten sonnets in the 1645 volume only 'How soon hath time the subtle theef of youth' is a masterpiece, though the Nightingale sonnet and 'When the assault was intended to the city' are both fine of their kind.

During the seventeen years of his political activity, Milton cultivated the sonnet because he had neither the time nor the energy to devote to longer flights. At times, indeed, he seemed to have completely exhausted his poetic vein, and then he produced his intolerably flat versions of seventeen of the psalms. These were exercises in patience rather than in poetry. The later sonnets are of various kinds—satirical (those on the divorce controversy), complimentary (those addressed to Lawes and Lawrence), a mixture of compliment and politics (those written to Fairfax, Vane, and Cromwell), political (On the new forcers of Conscience, On the late Massacre in Piedmont) and personal (the memorial sonnets on his wife and Mrs. Thomason, and the two sonnets on his blindness). At least ten of these later sonnets are masterly. They are, in the best sense of the word, *occasional* poems; but they possess a force and concentration which is partly due to the damming up of his poetic energies.

The public ones are, as Wordsworth said, 'soul-animating strains'. The sonnets to Fairfax and Cromwell are totally without servility. Milton gives us what is almost an objective statement of their great deeds and then reminds them of their equally great duties—to win the victories of peace, to cleanse corruption in high places, and to preserve freedom of conscience from the secular chains of a State Church. The sonnet on the massacre in Piedmont shows us Milton in his sternest Old Testament mood, and those to Lawrence and Skinner in his most Horatian and amiable. The most moving sonnets are the three on his blindness, particularly perhaps the restrained pathos of the one in which he dreams of seeing his dead wife.

The sonnets have very little imagery; and what there is is comparatively conventional. Milton obtains his impressive effect by piling clause on clause, by accommodating what he has to say to the sonnet-form, with no padding, and no sense of strain, by the superb organization of his matter, and by a monumental and sometimes epigrammatic precision of statement. In his method he seems to have been influenced by the 'heroic' sonnets of Della Casa. It is no accident that several lines have become familiar quotations:

> For what can Warr, but endless Warr still breed?
> Peace hath her victories
> No less renownd than warr.
> *New Presbyter* is but *Old Priest* writ Large.
> They also serve who only stand and waite.
> I wak'd, she fled, and day brought back my night.

Shakespeare's sonnets are, at their best, more richly poetical, more sensuously alive, the best of Words-

worth's are almost as fine as Milton's, and some by
Gerard Manley Hopkins exhibit an even greater concentration and some spiritual qualities we may value
above Milton's; but in any collection of the greatest
English sonnets Milton would be represented by at least
six.

Chapter Seven

THE LAST PERIOD

ON the eve of the Restoration Milton had every excuse for accepting the inevitable. He had devoted the past twenty years of his life to political and religious controversy, he had sacrificed his eyes in defending the British people; and the parties and leaders in whom he had put his trust had failed to establish the good society. Other republicans, realizing that their cause was lost and that they could continue the struggle only at the risk of their lives, one by one fell silent. But Milton, disregarding his own safety and jeopardizing his chance of fulfilling his poetic ambitions, continued to plead against the restoration of the monarchy and warned his readers against the calamities inseparable from foreign or domestic slavery:

> What I have spoken, is the Language of that which is not called amiss *The good Old Cause*: if it seem strange to any, it will not seem more strange, I hope, than convincing to Backsliders. Thus much I should perhaps have said, though I were sure I should have spoken only to Trees and Stones; and had none to cry to, but with the Prophet, O Earth, Earth, Earth! to tell the very soil itself, what her perverse inhabitants are deaf to. Nay, though what I have spoke, should happen (which Thou suffer not, who didst create Mankind free; nor Thou next, who didst redeem us from being Servants of Men!) to be the last words of our expiring Liberty.

Most poets changed with the times. Cowley hastened to atone for his 'collaboration' with a long Ode on the

Restoration which is composed of bombast and blasphemy. Waller had written a panegyric and an elegy on Cromwell and yet was one of the first to celebrate the return of Charles II. Dryden hastened to expiate his *Heroick Stanzas* written in memory of Cromwell with three poems addressed to his sacred majesty, Charles II. Marvell, who might with decency have reverted to his early royalism, remained constant to his principles. But Milton was in a more dangerous position. He had been an apologist of the Regicides, and he was hated as the author of *Eikonoklastes*. He wisely went into hiding for a few months until the passing of the Act of Oblivion; but two of his books were burnt by the common hangman, and he himself was imprisoned for a while. He was saved from the scaffold, partly by Marvell's agitation on his behalf behind the scenes, partly by the fact that some Royalists admired his poetry and that he was known to have helped both D'avenant and the grandson of Spenser during the Commonwealth period, and partly, no doubt, because the sparing of the blind rebel might be regarded as an example of extraordinary clemency. According to one story Milton was actually offered state employment under the government he hated, but he contemptuously refused.

Yet his position was tragic. He had lost most of his savings. He was a widower, unloved by two of his daughters and cheated by his servants. He was defeated, hated, and blind. The cause to which he had sacrificed his poetry was irreparably lost; and, in spite of his patriotism, he complained to a friend that he was left without a country. He seems to have gone in fear of assassination at the hands of the Sons of Belial, the unruly Royalists who resented his escape from the scaffold. Some of his closest political associates had been executed, and the bodies of the regicides had been treated with barbarous indignity.

Milton therefore dedicated what he regarded as his best and richest possession, *Christian Doctrine*, not to his fellow-countrymen, but to Protestants everywhere. He had hoped that the Puritan Revolution and the reform of the Reformation might serve as an example to the rest of Europe, and that England might become a leader of the Protestant powers. Now with the collapse of the Commonwealth he addressed himself to an international audience, though the work was not actually published until 1825. Mr. J. Middleton Murry has argued that 'Milton's Protestant theology ended in a complete emancipation from Christianity itself.' The truth of this statement depends on our interpretation of Christianity; but we may admit that Milton had little sense of the sacramental element in religion, and that the method employed in *Christian Doctrine* leads naturally if imperceptibly to modernism and even rationalism. To us, however, the treatise, though a greater feat for a blind man even than the three great poems of Milton's final period, is chiefly interesting for the light which it throws on the theology of *Paradise Lost*. In his epic Milton was deliberately inexplicit with regard to his numerous heresies.

It is significant that in his last years Milton had broken with all religious sects. As Toland tells us:

He ever exprest the profoundest Reverence to the Deity as well in Deeds as Words; and would say to his Friends, that the divine Properties of Goodness, Justice, and Mercy, were the adequat Rule of human Actions, nor less the Object of Imitation for privat Advantages, than of Admiration or Respect for their own Excellence and Perfection. In his early days he was a Favorer of those Protestants then opprobriously cal'd by the name of *Puritans*: In his middle years he was best pleas'd with the *Independents* and *Anabaptists*, as allowing of more Liberty than others, and coming nearest in his opinion to the primitive practice: but in the latter part

of his Life, he was not a profest Member of any particular
Sect among Christians, he frequented none of their Assemblies, nor made use of their peculiar Rites in his Family.
Whether this proceded from a dislike of their uncharitable
and endless Disputes, and that Love of Dominion, or In-
clination to Persecution, which, he said, was a piece of
Popery inseparable from all Churches; or whether he
thought one might be a good Man, without subscribing to any
Party: and that they had all in som things corrupted the
Institutions of Jesus Christ, I will by no means adventure to
determine.

It is not an accident that one of his closest friends in these
years was Dr. Nathaniel Paget, who possessed a large
collection of Socinian books, and that he was particularly
kind to the young Quaker, Thomas Ellwood. He, like
the Friends, had always relied on the Inner Light; and in
his last years there was not much else on which in religious matters he did rely.

The last fourteen years of his life were spent partly in
London, and partly at Chalfont St. Giles, to which he
retired during the Plague in 1665. It was Ellwood who
found 'a pretty box' for Milton in this Buckinghamshire
village. He had been introduced to the poet a few years
earlier by Dr. Paget—Isaac Pennington being a mutual
friend—and he took lodgings near Milton's house in
London so that he could read to him in Latin every week-
day afternoon. Milton insisted on his acquiring the continental pronunciation, and when he showed by his reading that he did not fully understand a passage Milton
interpreted it for him. The sequel at Chalfont is one of
the best-known incidents in Milton's biography. Ellwood, released from gaol, visited the poet:

After some common Discourses had passed between us, he
called for a Manuscript of his; which being brought he
delivered it to me, bidding me take it home with me, and

read it at my Leisure: and when I had so done, return it to him, with my Judgment thereupon. When I came home, and had set myself to read it, I found it was that Excellent Poem, which he entituled *Paradise Lost*. After I had, with the best Attention, read it through, I made him another Visit, and returned him his Book, with due Acknowledgement of the Favour he had done me, in Communicating it to me. He asked me how I liked it, and what I thought of it; which I modestly, but freely told him: and after some further Discourse about it, I pleasantly said to him, Thou hast said much here of *Paradise Lost*; but what hast thou to say on Paradise found? He made me no Answer, but sate some time in a Muse: then brake off that Discourse, and fell upon another Subject.

Milton must have been somewhat taken aback, since he had dealt with the recovery of paradise in his original epic; but some years later, when Ellwood visited him in London, he showed him the manuscript of *Paradise Regain'd*, saying in a pleasant tone: 'This is owing to you: for you put it into my Head, by the Question you put to me at Chalfont; which before I had not thought of.'

Milton had lost his Bread Street house in the Great Fire and when he came back to London he lived in a small house in the parish of St. Giles, Cripplegate. He had married for the third time in 1663: he needed a housekeeper, and his daughters urgently needed a stepmother. His bride, Elizabeth Minshull, the daughter of a Cheshire farmer and a relation of Dr. Paget, was twenty-four years of age, pretty and golden-haired; and though according to one story she was a termagant and unkind to her step-daughters, the weight of the evidence suggests that she made a good and affectionate wife. She protected the poet from the unkindness of his daughters, earning the dislike of two of them, and from the depradations of a servant who had been encouraged by the daughters to embezzle the housekeeping money. She took pains to give the poet the dishes he most enjoyed, a matter of importance to a blind man. One day at dinner he told her affectionately: 'God have mercy, Betty, I see thou wilt perform according to thy promise in providing me such dishes as I think fit whilst I live, and when I die thou knowest I have left thee all.' After his death she treasured his portraits, his tobacco box, copies of *Paradise Lost* and *Paradise Regain'd*, and letters written to him by distinguished foreigners; and she remained on good terms with Deborah, to whom she gave the poet's seal and other relics. She returned to Nantwich, where her entertaining was said to be economical. 'Like Mrs. Milton's feasts', the saying went, 'enough and no more.'

The poet's daughters, if not exactly Gonerils, were far from being Cordelias. In spite of Edward Phillips's story, confirmed by Deborah in her old age, it is difficult to believe that she and Mary were made to read to their father in languages of which they were totally ignorant—Hebrew, Greek, Italian, Spanish and French. Anne, we are told, was excused this task because of her indistinct speech. She seems to have been of subnormal intelligence, besides being a cripple. As Phillips admits, there were plenty of friends who were glad of the opportunity of reading to the poet. Deborah, years later, could recite passages of Latin poetry, and it is possible that Milton made an unsuccessful attempt to teach his daughters some foreign languages, or he may have felt that they ought to earn their keep. The experiment was finally abandoned, and Milton used to remark sardonically that 'one tongue was enough for a woman'. As the daughters proved to be useless or unco-operative he sent them to learn the craft of lace-making, so that they would not be unprovided for when he died. Deborah became a paid companion to a lady in Dublin, and there married Abraham Clarke, variously described as a weaver, a mercer, and a silk-merchant, without her father's knowledge.

The poet decided to leave his daughters only their mother's still unpaid dowry. It is clear that all three daughters felt closer to the Powell family than they did to their father, and to him they behaved undutifully, as he felt. Mary, on hearing of his proposal to marry Elizabeth Minshull, exclaimed to a servant, 'that that was no news to hear of his marriage, but if she should hear of his death that was something.' There is little doubt that the elder girls behaved badly, even selling some of their father's precious books; but some of the blame must lie with Milton himself who had failed to win either the girls' love or their dutifulness. It is therefore pleasant to know that Deborah in her old age seems to have borne her father no ill-will. She had, unlike the others, acted as his amanuensis, and when she was visited by enquirers just before she died she spoke of him with great tenderness.

> She said He was Delightful Company, the Life of the Conversation, and That on Account of a Flow of Subject, and an Unaffected Chearfulness and Civility.

She may have felt that this kind of reminiscence would be more acceptable than an account of family wrangling; but there is no mistaking the genuineness of her cry on being shown his portrait in crayons:

> 'Tis My Father, 'tis my Dear Father! I see him! 'tis Him! and then She put her Hands to several Parts of Her Face, 'tis the very Man! Here, Here——

It appears that Milton's nephews were closer to him than his daughters, and Edward Phillips picked his uncle's brains for his *Theatrum Poetarum* and other works. He acted as the poet's literary executor and published the *Letters of State* with a biographical account of the author.

The other nephew, John, had written a Latin defence of Milton in 1652 and a *Satyr against Hypocrites* in 1655; and though Milton may have regretted some things in this satire, he agreed with the sentiments expressed in it. He would not have approved of the indecencies of *Sportive Art*, but it is not likely that he knew of this book or of the travesty of Virgil, published in 1673, in which Harrison, Bradshaw and Vane, three of the men he most admired, appeared in Hell. But at about the same time John Phillips acted as the poet's amanuensis, copying out some sonnets for the augmented edition of the *Poems*; and, as Miss Darbishire has argued, he may have been the author of the affectionate and admiring anonymous life misused by Wood in his biography. It says much for Milton's tolerance and good nature that he retained an affection for his scapegrace nephew; and it says even more for him that this nephew displays such genuine admiration and affection for the old Puritan. It is significant that both nephews thought that he had behaved generously to Mary Powell.

Paradise Lost, delayed by the Plague and the Fire, was finally published in 1667. Seven years later a second edition appeared, with two of the longer books divided into two so as to make the traditional twelve books. *Paradise Regain'd* and *Samson Agonistes* appeared in one volume in 1671. After the completion of his three major poems, Milton spent his last few years in preparing an enlarged edition of his minor poems, and he included early poems excluded from the 1645 volume as well as others written between 1645 and 1656; he prepared for publication *The History of Britain*, written long before; and he consented to the publication of his Latin letters—his official correspondence had to be excluded—and his undergraduate prolusions (1674). Once, in the year before he died, he ventured again into political controversy. By the Declaration of Indulgence Charles II was proposing to emancipate the Catholics by tolerating Nonconformists. Marvell at this time was engaged in a campaign for the toleration of all Protestant sects, and it was perhaps at his suggestion that Milton wrote *Of True Religion*. For various reasons Milton did not extend his toleration to Catholics. He still thought that their political allegiance might be divided, he felt that as they did not base their beliefs on the Bible alone they were in a different category from all Protestant sects, and above all he was rightly suspicious of Charles II's motives. The rest of the pamphlet is a last plea for the toleration which was always near Milton's heart:

> It is a human frailty to err, and no man is infallible here on earth. . . . How unequal, how uncharitable must it needs be, to impose that which his conscience cannot urge him to impose, upon him whose conscience forbids him to obey!

He admits that there should be no fundamental division in the Church.

> It should be so indeed; yet seams in the same cloth neither hurt the garment nor misbecome it; and not only seams, but schisms will be while men are fallible.

Finally, he has a last fling at the immorality of the new age:

> The last means to avoid popery is, to amend our lives. It is a general complaint, that this nation of late years is grown more numerously and excessively vicious than heretofore; pride, luxury, drunkenness, whoredom, cursing, swearing, bold and open atheism everywhere abounding: where these grow, no wonder if popery also grows apace.

Milton's life in these last years followed a quiet routine. He rose at four o'clock, and a man read to him out of the Hebrew Bible. 'Then he contemplated. At 7 his

man came to him again and then read to him and wrote
till dinner: the writing was as much as the reading.'
After dinner he used to walk in the garden for several
hours. Sometimes he used a swing for exercise. In the
evening he read poetry or played on the organ or bass
viol. He retired to bed about nine o'clock. Before this
time, while he was writing his last three great poems, he
used to compose early in the morning, sometimes as
many as thirty lines. If his amanuensis arrived late, he
used to complain, saying 'hee wanted to bee milkd.' He
seldom wrote verse in the summer:

> All the time of writing his *Paradise Lost*, his veine began at the
> Autumnal Æquinoctiall and ceased at the Vernall or there-
> abouts (I believe about May).

When he was dictating 'he Sat leaning Backward
Obliquely in an Easy Chair, with his Leg flung over the
Elbow of it'. He was 'extreme pleasant in his conversation' at meal-times, but, Aubrey adds, 'Satyricall'.
According to Dryden he pronounced the letter R very
hard, 'a certaine signe of a satyricall wit'. In later years
'he was visited much by learned: more than he did
desire.' To these details, mostly from Aubrey, we can
add John Phillips's account of his appearance:

> Hee was of a moderate Stature, and well proportion'd, of a
> ruddy Complexion, light brown Hair, and handsom
> Features; save that his Eyes were none of the quickest. His
> deportment was sweet and affable; and his Gate erect and
> Manly, bespeaking Courage and undauntedness (or a Nil
> conscire). On which account hee wore a Sword while hee
> had his Sight, and was skill'd in using it. Hee had an excel-
> lent Ear, and could bear a part both in Vocal and Instru-
> mental Music.

In his later years, at least, he rarely drank between meals.
But, according to Edward Phillips, in the days before his
first marriage he would once a month

drop into the Society of some Young Sparks of his Acquaintance, the chief whereof were Mr. *Alphry*, and Mr. *Miller*, two Gentlemen of *Gray's-Inn*, the *Beau's* of those Times, but nothing near so bad as those now-a-days; with these Gentlemen he would so far make bold with his Body, as now and then to keep a Gawdy-day.

The passage is worth quoting, if only to qualify the popular conception of Milton as severely puritanical in his habits. His early biographers are unanimous in stressing his affability, his generosity, and his equanimity of temper. Although he was severe with his pupils—the Earl of Barrimore and Sir Thomas Gardner soon sought a less exacting tutor—he was 'most familiar and free in his conversation' with them out of school hours. In his last years he enjoyed the visits of his friends, who included Marvell, Paget and two booksellers, Thomason and Millington. Once he was visited by the poet of the new age. John Dryden asked his permission to turn *Paradise Lost* into his operatic *State of Innocence*. Milton consented good-humouredly, saying, 'It seems you have a mind to tag my points, and you have my leave to tag 'em.' Marvell evidently alludes to this story in his verses on *Paradise Lost*:

> Well mightest thou scorn thy Readers to allure
> With tinkling Rhime, of thy own sense secure;
> While the *Town-Bayes* writes all the while and spells.
> And like a Pack-horse tires without his Bells.

Like his father, Milton suffered from the gout, and in his later years he was often in great pain; but during the attacks he used to sing. Jonathan Richardson gives a composite account of Milton towards the end of his life:

One that had Often seen him, told me he us'd to come to a House where He Liv'd, and he has also Met him in the Street, Led by *Millington*, the same who was so Famous an

Auctioneer of Books about the time of the Revolution, and Since. . . . This was 3 or 4 Years before he Dy'd. He then wore no Sword that My Informer remembers, though Probably he did, at least 'twas his Custom not long before to wear one with a Small Silver-Hilt, and in Cold Weather a Grey Camblet Coat. . . . The Fashion of the Coat Then was not Much Unlike what the Quakers Wear Now.

I have heard many Years Since that he Us'd to Sit in a Grey Coarse Cloath Coat at the Door of his House, near *Bun-hill* Fields Without *Moor-gate*, in Warm Sunny Weather to Enjoy the Fresh Air, and So, as well as in his Room, received the Visits of People of Distinguish'd Parts, as well as Quality. And very Lately I had the Good Fortune to have Another Picture of him from an Ancient Clergy-man in *Dorsetshire*, *Dr. Wright*; He found him in a Small House, he thinks but One Room on a Floor; in That, up One pair of Stairs, which was hung with a Rusty Green, he found *John Milton*, Sitting in an Elbow Chair, Black Cloaths, and Neat enough, Pale, but not Cadaverous, his Hands and Fingers Gouty, and with Chalk Stones. Among Other Discourses He exprest Himself to This Purpose; that was he Free from the Pain This gave him, his Blindness would be Tolerable.

He died quietly on 8 November, 1674, with 'so little pain or emotion that the time of his expiring was not perceived by those in the room.' He was buried in St. Giles, Cripplegate, in his father's grave. In 1790 his coffin was broken open and his remains exhibited to sightseers, who bought locks of hair and even his teeth—more teeth, perhaps, than he had possessed in his lifetime. But by this time he had taken his place amongst the greatest of English poets.

Chapter Eight

PARADISE LOST

As early as 1638 Milton had told Manso of his ambition to write an epic poem about King Arthur. In the elegy on Diodati he was still meditating an *Arthuriad*, perhaps in stanzas like *The Faerie Queene* and Tasso's *Jerusalem Delivered*. Two years later, in a famous digression in *The Reason of Church Government*, he described his poetic ambitions. He hoped to 'leave something so written to aftertimes, as they should not willingly let die.' He goes on to consider the various possibilities: an epic poem 'whereof the two poems of Homer and those other two of Virgil and Tasso are a diffuse, and the book of Job a brief model', a play in the Greek manner, or 'magnific odes and hymns' in the manner of Pindar or Callimachus. He debated moreover whether to write an epic according to Aristotle's rules or to follow nature, and what pre-conquest hero he might choose as the pattern of a Christian hero. Such a programme, as Milton quite realized, could not be accomplished in a few years, or indeed by a single poet. It was 'not to be raised from the heat of youth or the vapours of wine,' like the love poems of the Cavaliers. It could not even 'be obtained by the invocation of Dame Memory and her siren daughters', but only

by devout prayer to that eternal spirit who can enrich with all utterance and knowledge, and sends out His seraphim with the hallowed fire of His altar to touch and purify the lips of whom He pleases: to this must be added industrious and select reading, steady observation, insight into all seemly and generous arts and affairs, till which in some measure be compassed, at mine own peril and cost I refuse not to sustain this expectation from as many as are not loath to hazard so much credulity upon the best pledges that I can give them.

It has been necessary to quote this passage since it is the main key to the understanding of Milton's poetic ambitions. He wanted to write poetry which, if not directly didactic, would serve to teach delightfully. He was animated by moral, religious, and patriotic motives; he thought he could best serve his country by putting before it noble and religious ideals in the highest poetic form; and he believed that he could best serve his God by following his vocation as a poet. It is noteworthy that he wishes to satisfy traditional literary demands and also to satisfy himself that he had good scriptural precedents. He appealed not only to Homer, but also to the book of Job, not only to Sophocles but also to the Song of Solomon, not only to Pindar, but to the lyric poetry of the Bible. He eventually accomplished the diffuse epic, *Paradise Lost*, on the model of Virgil rather than of Spenser, the brief epic in the shape of *Paradise Regain'd*, and the tragedy on the Greek model, *Samson Agonistes*. It might be argued that such poems as the 'Ode on the Morning of Christ's Nativity' and 'At a Solemn Music' belonged to the category of 'magnific odes and hymns'. But though Milton quoted classical models, and though he was still dallying with the idea of a British epic— 'what king or knight, before the conquest, might be chosen'—in the end he chose in each case a Biblical subject.

About the same time as Milton outlined his poetic ambitions for the general public he jotted down for his private use some hundred subjects which might serve as the basis of a dramatic poem. Thirty-three are taken from British history, which he had been studying intensively, and these included Macbeth, but not King Arthur. He had apparently decided that Arthur was legendary rather than historical, and he wished to write a poem which was historically as well as allegorically true, though there may have been another list of epic subjects in which Arthur was included.

The rest of the subjects were Biblical, mostly from the Old Testament; they included the death of Samson, and no less than four plans for a tragedy on the Fall of Man. Two of these consisted merely of a list of characters. A third divided the subject into five acts. The fourth, entitled *Adam Unparadiz'd*, consists of a full scenario:

> The angel Gabriel, either descending or entering, shewing since this globe was created, his frequency as much on earth, as in heavn, describes Paradise, next the Chorus shewing the reason of his comming to keep his watch in Paradise after Lucifers rebellion by command from god, & withall expressing his desire to see, & know more concerning this excellent new creature man. the angel Gabriel as by his name signifying a prince of power tracing paradise with a more free office passes by the station of the chorus & desired by them relates what he knew of man, as the creation of Eve with thire love, & mariage.
>
> after this Lucifer appeares after his overthrow, bemoans himself, seeks revenge on man. the Chorus prepare resistance at his first approach, at last after discourse of enmity on either side he departs wherat the chorus sings of the battell, & victorie in heavn against him & accomplices as before after the first act was sung a hymn of the creation.
>
> heer again may appear Lucifer relating, & insulting in what he had don to the destruction of man. man next & Eve having by this time bin seduc't by the serpent appeares confusedly cover'd with leaves. conscience in a shape accuses him, Justice cites him to the place whither Jehova call'd for

him. in the mean while the chorus entertains the stage, &
his [sic] inform'd by some angel the manner of his fall. heer
the chorus bewailes Adams fall.

Adam then & Eve returne, accuse one another but
especially Adam layes the blame to his wife, is stubborn in
his offence. Justice appeares [to] reason with him, con-
vinces him. the chorus admonisheth Adam & bids him
beware by Lucifers example of impenitence.

the Angel is sent to banish them out of paradise but before
causes to passe before his eyes in shapes a mask of all the
evils of this life & world. he is humbled, relents, dispaires.
at last appeares Mercy, comforts him, promises the Messiah,
then calls in faith, hope, & charity, instructs him. he
repents gives god the glory, submitts to his penalty. the
chorus breifly concludes.

Milton is said to have seen a performance of Andreini's
Adamo, and he had certainly read it. He may have wished
to follow up the success of *Comus* with a Biblical play
which would serve to counteract the Puritan opposition
to the secular drama and, as Hanford has suggested, he
may have hoped with the assistance of Henry Lawes to
write plays with music. Certainly in *The Reason of Church
Government* he argued that it was the duty of the State to
provide culture and recreation for its citizens, including
'wise and artful recitations sweetened with eloquent and
graceful enticements to the love and practice of justice,
temperance and fortitude'; and he suggested that the
magistrates should stage plays 'in Theatres, porches, or
what other place or way may win most upon the people
to receive at once both recreation and instruction'.

According to two of Milton's early biographers, he
actually began a drama on the Fall of Man, about the time
of his marriage. The speech of Satan in *Paradise Lost*,
Book IV, is said to have been the opening speech of the
drama:

O thou that, with surpassing Glory crownd,
Look'st from thy sole Dominion like the God
Of this new World; at whose sight all the starrs
Hide thir diminsht heads; to thee I call,
But with no friendly voice, and add thy name
O Sun, to tell thee how I hate thy beams . . .

If this is correct, Milton had departed from his scenario
in which Satan does not appear till the second act.

The poem was then abandoned for sixteen years.
Milton's matrimonial difficulties, his pamphleteering,
and his political duties intervened; and when he took up
the subject again, he recast his material in the form of an
epic. The poem as we have it was begun in 1658 and
finished in 1663. Milton spent a year or two on revision,
and the Great Fire and the Plague delayed publication
until 1667.

It will be obvious from Milton's early scenario that if
Paradise Lost had been written fifteen years before it
would have been a very different poem. It would have
been nearer to *Comus* in form and style than the poem he
actually wrote; and those who deplore the later development of Milton's blank-verse and what they regard as the
hardening of his sensibility may regret that he allowed so
many years to elapse. The Milton of 1660 was in some
ways narrower and harsher than the man who charmed
the academies of Italy, and his activities as a political
propagandist and his virtual abandonment of poetry for
nearly twenty years were dangerous if not disastrous. Yet
there were compensations. In 1640 Milton believed in
original sin and the Fall of Man, but the belief was merely
a formal article of his creed: it had not been 'proved
upon his pulses'. The great shock to Wordsworth's
moral nature, the conflict between patriotism and revo-
lutionary idealism, had the effect, once he had begun to
recover, of turning him into a great poet. Milton's first

shock came when he was much older than Wordsworth, with the initial breakdown of his first marriage. A second shock, perhaps as grave, came with the reception accorded to what he regarded as the sweet reasonableness of his divorce pamphlets. This was followed by his progressive political disillusionment with his fellow-countrymen, which culminated in the Restoration and the execution of some of his associates. On top of all this there was his blindness.

The Fall of Man had become not one possible subject among many: it was now the one theme which was perfectly suited to Milton's ideas, experience, and talents. The examination of the corruption of man's heart was a necessity for the poet; he wished to explain why human nature had come short of his expectations, why all his hopes had been frustrated. It was a subject too in which his genius had most scope, and in which his limitations as a poet could be turned to advantage. His passionate interest in theological and political questions and his lack of that understanding of individual human beings, which comes (as Eliot remarks) from 'an affectionate observation of men and women', were a positive advantage in writing of Adam and Eve. They had to be prototypes of Man and Woman, and (as Eliot says again) 'were they more particularized they would be false, and if Milton had been more interested in humanity, he could not have created them'.

There are many passages in *Paradise Lost* which reveal Milton's personal feelings. At the opening of Book VII he writes of his own situation at the time of the Restoration, fallen on evil days, encompassed with dangers, and hating the revellers of Charles II's court:

> Standing on Earth, not rapt above the Pole,
> More safe I Sing, with mortal voice unchang'd
> To hoarce or mute, though fall'n on evil dayes,

On evil dayes though fall'n, and evil tongues;
In darkness, and with dangers compast round,
And solitude; yet not alone, while thou
Visit'st my slumbers Nightly, or when Morn
Purples the East: still govern thou my Song,
Urania, and fit audience find, though few.
But drive farr off the barbarous dissonance
Of *Bacchus* and his Revellers, the Race
Of that wilde Rout that tore the *Thracian* Bard
In *Rhodope*, where Woods and Rocks had Eares
To rapture, till the savage clamor dround
Both Harp and Voice; nor could the Muse defend
Her Son.

Scattered through the poem are a number of passages expressing the sentiments of Milton's political pamphlets. In the last book, for example, when Michael tells Adam that because of his fall true liberty is lost, Milton seems to be blaming the failure of the Commonwealth on original sin. As in many of his works in prose and verse he maintains that only the man who is able to rule his passions can be genuinely free:

true Libertie
Is lost, which alwayes with right Reason dwells
Twinn'd, and from her hath no dividual being:
Reason in man obscur'd, or not obey'd,
Immediately inordinate desires
And upstart Passions catch the Government
From Reason, and to servitude reduce
Man till then free. Therefore since hee permits
Within himself unworthie Powers to reign
Over free Reason, God in Judgement just
Subjects him from without to violent Lords;
Who oft as undeservedly enthrall
His outward freedom: Tyrannie must be,
Though to the Tyrant thereby no excuse.
Yet somtimes Nations will decline so low

From vertue, which is reason, that no wrong,
But Justice, and some fatal curse annext
Deprives them of thir outward libertie,
Thir inward lost.

Milton, as has often been remarked, was in *Paradise Lost*
not only justifying God's ways to men; he was justifying
His ways to Englishmen between 1640 and 1660. He
was telling them why they had failed to establish the
good society, why they had welcomed back the monarchy.
They had failed through their own weakness, their own
lack of faith, their own passions and greed, their own
sin. God was not to blame.

Chateaubriand remarked that Cromwell and his
associates served as Milton's models for his portraits of
the infernal crew. This, of course, is absurd: but it is
probably true that the debate in hell would have been
lacking in power and verisimilitude if the poet had not
lived through the period of the Long Parliament. A
knowledge of political debate and the arts of the political
pamphleteer were as necessary a part of Milton's equip-
ment as his continued absorption in theological discussion, as evidenced by *Christian Doctrine*; and with almost
any other subject for his epic these things would have
been grave limitations.

Some critics have gone further and argued that Milton
was getting his own back on his first wife in his portrait of
Eve, though Eve is not unsympathetically portrayed
within the limits imposed by the fable; and many critics
have claimed that Milton, who was a defeated rebel,
unconsciously identified himself with Satan. But the
Good Old Cause, whatever our political views, can
scarcely be identified with the infernal cause; and it is
difficult to believe that Milton, even unconsciously,
identified the two. Blake, in *The Marriage of Heaven and
Hell*, has often been quoted in support of this view, but

his famous dictum that Milton 'was a true Poet and of the Devil's party without knowing it' means something quite different in its context. Blake was arguing that 'without contraries is no progression', that Reason and Energy are both necessary to human existence, that 'Good is the passive that obeys Reason, Evil is the active springing from Energy'. In this framework it is natural that Blake should make the Devil assert that 'The reason Milton wrote in fetters when he wrote of Angels and God, and at liberty when of Devils and Hell, is because he was a true Poet and of the Devil's party without knowing it'. Blake's brilliant paradoxes must be considered in relation to the whole content of *The Marriage of Heaven and Hell* and, indeed, to his general method of dialectic in his prophetic books; but this particular statement means, at least in part, that poetry is emotional rather than rational in origin, and Blake, as far as the literary application of the remark is concerned, is as orthodox as Wordsworth who said a few years later that poetry was the spontaneous overflow of powerful feelings.

Nevertheless, Mr. R. J. Z. Werblowsky, who is a disciple of Jung, argues forcibly in *Lucifer and Prometheus* that Milton himself unconsciously proceeded from the same assumption as Blake:

> That energy and creative vitality are Promethean and thus devilish, whilst Christ is reason and his lesson is passivity, obedience, and self-restraint.

Satan contains Promethean elements, no doubt, as Shelley also recognized, and Milton no longer possessed the optimistic humanism of his youth; but Mr. Werblowsky, I believe, exaggerates the extent to which Milton was 'distrustful of our exploring and inventive energies', or represented 'the spirit of cultural asceticism and negation' at the time he wrote *Paradise Lost*. The remark is more applicable to *Paradise Regain'd*. There was, of course, a conflict in the seventeenth century, as there had been, for example, in Marlowe's *Doctor Faustus*—and Milton to some extent embodied it—between religious faith and a belief in the limitless possibilities of the advancement of knowledge for the emancipation of man; but to Milton, at every stage of his development, knowledge was a means to know God better rather than a means of enabling man to do without Him. It is true, as Werblowsky points out, that Milton's devils are great inventors, artists, musicians, and philosophers, that Raphael warns Adam against the untrammelled use of reason; but we are not to assume from this that Milton was condemning outright the fact of the Renaissance, together with the music and poetry he loved and the speculation in which he engaged. Nor can it be said that the poem is a failure because of the tension in Milton's mind between Puritanism and Humanism: without this tension the poem would have been lacking in complexity. If it had been written entirely from the standpoint of a puritanical hatred of the world, it would have been a failure as poetry; and if it had been written from the standpoint of humanist tradition it would have lacked the desperate sense of high seriousness necessary to the theme of the Fall of Man.

The obvious models for an epic poet in the seventeenth century were Virgil, Tasso, Ariosto, Camoens, and Spenser. Just as Virgil had glorified Rome and Camoens Portugal, so Milton had considered the possibilities of an Arthuriad; but he had written a substitute for a national epic in his *Defence of the English People*. He decided instead to write what may be regarded as an international epic, though he wrote it in English, and not in the Latin which he might have chosen. He rejected the loose episodic strucure of Ariosto and Spenser, and accepted

instead the Virgilian form. He rejected the stanzas used
by Spenser, the Italian poets and Camoens, but he must
have seriously considered whether to use the Spenserian
stanza; and since he thought that Spenser was a better
teacher than St. Thomas Aquinas he was in some danger
of writing an allegorical epic. We can see, indeed, from
poems as early as the Nativity Ode and as late as *Paradise
Regain'd* that he was a reader of the works of Giles and
Phineas Fletcher. *Christ's Victory and Triumph, The Purple
Island* and *Locustae* all influenced him. The first of these
poems, by Giles Fletcher, dealt with Christ's victory over
Satan in the wilderness, and His triumph over death on
the cross; and the fourth part, describing the joys of
heaven, formed a model, as we have seen, for parts of
'Lycidas' and 'Damon'. *The Purple Island* equally left its
mark on 'Lycidas'. *Locustae* contains an account of Satan,
which appears to have influenced the first two books of
Paradise Lost. These three poems, apart from the Latin
part of *Locustae*, were written in stanzas; but Milton
finally rejected both the form and the method of Spenserian allegory. D'avenant had proved by the very weakness of *Gondibert* that the quatrain was an unsuitable form
for an epic, but the couplet was becoming the standard
vehicle for long poems other than plays. It had been used
by Sylvester in his *Divine Weeks*, a translation of Du
Bartas's *La Sepmaine*, admired by Milton as a child, and,
as Professor G. C. Taylor has shown, this translation influenced *Paradise Lost* in certain details. It was popular,
especially with Puritans, and it belonged to a popular
genre, the hexameron. There were commentaries on the
six days of the Creation, and they inspired numerous
European epic poems which (Rajan tells us) were all intolerably dull.

But it should be said that Sylvester's translation is
sometimes excellent. The description of Eden, for

example, may well have caught Milton's eye, and the temptation of Eve perhaps formed the basis of Milton's more brilliant account. It must be admitted, however, that Sylvester often deserves Dryden's remark that he wrote 'abominable fustian'.

The couplet had been used too in Denham's translation of some books of the *Æneid*; and also by Cowley, whom Milton is said to have regarded as the best English poet after Shakespeare and Spenser, in his unfinished religious epic, *Davideis*, which was published just before Milton began to write *Paradise Lost*. It is clear from Marvell's commendatory verses, prefixed to the second edition of the poem, and from Milton's own defence of blank verse, that there had been some criticism of his final choice of that medium.

> The measure is *English* Heroic Verse without Rime, as that of *Homer* in *Greek*, and *Virgil* in *Latin*; Rime being no necessary Adjunct or true Ornament of Poem or good Verse, in longer Works especially, but the Invention of a barbarous Age, to set off wretched matter and lame Meeter; grac't indeed since by the use of some famous modern Poets, carried away by Custom, but much to thir own vexation, hindrance, and constraint to express many things otherwise, and for the most part worse than else they would have exprest them. Not without cause therefore some both *Italian* and *Spanish* Poets of prime note have rejected Rime both in longer and shorter Works, as have also long since our best *English* Tragedies, as a thing of it self, to all judicious eares, triveal and of no true musical delight; which consists only in apt Numbers, fit quantity of Syllables, and the sense variously drawn out from one Verse into another, not in the jingling sound of like endings, a fault avoyded by the learned Ancients both in Poetry and all good Oratory. This neglect then of Rime so little is to be taken for a defect, though it may seem so perhaps to vulgar Readers, that it rather is to be esteem'd an example set, the first in *English*, of ancient

liberty recover'd to Heroic Poem from the troublesom and modern bondage of Rimeing.

In *Comus*, as we have seen, Milton had rejected the more licentious blank verse of the Stuart dramatists for the more regular verse of the last years of the sixteenth century. For his epic the colloquial style of Massinger or Fletcher was even more obviously unsuitable. Nor would even the verse of Shakespeare's middle period have been a satisfactory model. A dramatist is bound, by the nature both of his form and of his audience, to give the illusion of actual conversation, even though he may be employing all the resources of rhetoric. The characters in an epic, on the other hand, are necessarily larger than life, not merely in the sense that Othello and Lear in the intensity of their passion tower above ordinary humanity, but in the sense that they are archetypal figures belonging usually to a remote period. Far from identifying ourselves with them as we read, we should regard them with awe and admiration as beings on another plane. There is no actor to mediate between poet and audience, and no actor could give a satisfactory performance in any of the great epic roles.

There is another and more important reason why the style of epic and tragedy must necessarily differ. As Mr. C. S. Lewis has pointed out, *Paradise Lost*, like the *Æneid* and unlike the *Iliad*, is an example of 'secondary' epic. The 'primary' epic was recited or chanted to the accompaniment of a musical instrument. The 'secondary' epic is normally read privately, and even though it may gain by being read aloud, there is no musical accompaniment. The poet, therefore, has to compensate for the lack of ceremony in the occasion by an elevation of style which will enable the reader to partake in the poetic ritual. It is futile to expect the nervous energy, the subtle involutions of style, the tentacular imagery, the linguistic

daring and the colloquial ease of Shakespeare's best verse.
It is not that Shakespeare uses English as a living language,
and Milton as a dead one. It is rather that with Shakespeare we witness the perpetual rebirth of language, and
that Milton employs a rigorously selective vocabulary and
a highly artificial rhythm for the deliberate purpose of
inducing in his readers a particular state of mind. Dr.
Leavis complains that

> reading *Paradise Lost* is a matter of resisting, of standing up
> against, the verse-movement, of subduing it into something
> tolerably like sensitiveness, and in the end our resistance is
> worn down; we surrender at last to the inescapable mono-
> tony of the ritual.

A few pages later he declares that Milton's magniloquence
'demands more deference than it merits' since 'mere oro-
tundity is a disproportionate part of the whole effect.'
The 'laboured, pedantic artifice of the diction' shows
that Milton is 'focusing rather upon words than upon per-
ceptions, sensations or things.' He 'exhibits a feeling *for*
words rather than a capacity for feeling through words.'
Milton's language is remote from 'any English that was
ever spoken', and the poet by his complete 'callousness
to the intrinsic nature of English . . . forfeits all possibility of subtle and delicate life in his verse.'

This is a powerful indictment, and however much we
disagree with it we should be grateful to Dr. Leavis for
acting as the Devil's advocate without knowing it. He
sees himself as a critical Abdiel who, almost alone has
stood for discrimination, sensibility and the creative
imagination against the deadly forces of academic sterility
and superstition. But although he may claim that he has
the later Keats and the early Eliot on his side, the poets
with these exceptions have been on the side of Milton.
Marvell and Dryden, Pope and Johnson, Wordsworth

K

and Coleridge, Tennyson, Arnold and Hopkins—to name
no others—all expressed a high admiration for Milton's
verse; and even Keats, in the act of shaking off Milton as
a model, would have been the last to deny his greatness.

It is difficult to substantiate the criticism that Milton
focuses on words rather than on sensations or things,
though too much praise of his organ-music and his love
of high-sounding proper names has somewhat confused
the issue. One passage quoted by Dr. Leavis from
'Lycidas' is a case in point:

> Or whether thou to our moist vows deny'd,
> Sleep'st by the fable of *Bellerus* old,
> Where the great vision of the guarded Mount
> Looks toward *Namancos* and *Bayona's* hold;
> Look homeward Angel now, and melt with ruth.

The sonorous proper names have a more precise function
than those used by Marlowe. *Bellerus* is derived from the
Roman name for Land's End. The reference to the
legend that the Archangel himself had appeared on St.
Michael's Mount carries the implication that he is guard-
ing England from foreign invasion—he is looking towards
the nearest point on the coast of Spain. But he is en-
joined to look homeward because of the danger not from
abroad but from the corrupted clergy 'then in their
height', and because of the death of one who might have
done something to stem the tide of corruption.

A passage in the first book of *Paradise Lost* well illustrates the function of the proper names which Milton
introduced from time to time:

> though all the Giant brood
> Of *Phlegra* with th'Heroic Race were joyn'd
> That fought at *Theb's* and *Ilium*, on each side
> Mixt with auxiliar Gods; and what resounds
> In Fable or *Romance* of *Uthers* Son

> Begirt with *British* and *Armoric* Knights;
> And all who since, Baptiz'd or Infidel
> Jousted in *Aspramont* or *Montalban*,
> *Damasco*, or *Marocco*, or *Trebisond*,
> Or whom Biserta sent from *Afric* shore
> When *Charlemain* with all his Peerage fell
> By *Fontarabbia*.

The names are sonorous, but they are also full of mean-
ing. Milton alludes to the war between Gods and Giants,
to Polynices and his six companions who fought against
Thebes in Æschylus's play, to the heroes of the *Iliad* and
of the Arthurian legend, to the Crusades and Tasso's
Gerusalemme Liberata, to Ariosto's *Orlando Furioso*, to
Rinaldo's castle of Montauban mentioned by Pulci and
Boiardo, to the battles between Moors and Spaniards,
and to the *Song of Roland* or some other version of the
Charlemagne cycle. The allusions to the poetry of
Greece, Italy, France and England help to place *Paradise
Lost* in the epic tradition.[1] It is significant that Milton
compares his devils to the heroes of previous epics, for he
believed that his subject was superior to that of all the
epics of the past. He was dealing with the greatest subject of all. It was truth, not fiction; and he was describing what he calls 'the better fortitude of Patience and
Heroic Martyrdom'. His argument, therefore, was

> Not less but more Heroic than the wrauth
> Of stern *Achilles* on his Foe pursu'd
> Thrice Fugitive about *Troy* Wall, or rage
> Of *Turnus* for *Lavinia* disespous'd,
> Or *Neptun's* ire or *Juno's* that so long
> Perplex'd the *Greek* and *Cytherea's* Son.

---

[1] R. R. Cawley, *Milton and the Literature of Travel* (1951), pp. 9–23, shows
that the geographical list in Book XI (370 ff.) is packed with meaning, and that
the names are not chosen primarily for their sound.

Another passage in Book I illustrates the function of the Miltonic simile:

> Angel Forms, who lay intrans't
> Thick as Autumnal Leaves that strow the Brooks
> In *Vallombrosa*, where th'*Etrurian* shades
> High overarch't imbowr; or scatterd sedge
> Afloat, when with fierce Winds *Orion* arm'd
> Hath vext the Red-Sea Coast, whose waves orethrew
> *Busiris* and his *Memphian* Chivalrie,
> While with perfidious hatred they pursu'd
> The Sojourners of *Goshen*, who beheld
> From the safe shore their floating Carkases
> And broken Chariot Wheels, so thick bestrown
> Abject and lost lay these, covering the Flood,
> Under amazement of their hideous change.

In the lines about Vallombrosa, Milton was doubtless referring to something he had seen on his Italian journey; but he was also alluding to a well-known simile in *Æneid* VI, describing the flocking of the ghosts in the underworld:

> *Quam multa in silvis auctumni frigore primo*
> *Lapsa cadunt folia.*

> Multidudinous as the leaves that fall in forests
> At the first frost of autumn . . .

lines which were echoed by Dante in the *Inferno*:

> *Come d'autumno si levan le foglie*
> *l'una appresso dell'altra, fin che 'l ramo*
> *vede alla terra tutte le sue spoglie.*

This allusion to two hell-scenes in previous epics enables Milton to recall to the reader once again the place of the poem in the European epic tradition, and by the specific reference to a place he had visited he makes the simile something more than a mere echo. The angels are

appropriately compared to dead leaves because both are
scattered on the water by decay and loss of vitality. The
reference to the miracle of the Red Sea is a reminder that
the Rebel Angels are evil and that God is omnipotent,
and both they and Pharaoh's troops have been overthrown
by God's intervention. For the strict purposes of comparison Milton need have said only that the hosts were as
thick as autumn leaves or floating sedge. But the remaining lines not merely add richness and link the poem with
its great predecessors: they also open a window on an
episode of Biblical history to which Milton returned in
his last book, and the similes are functional rather than
digressive or decorative.

Some of the long epic similes are less integral to the
theme of the poem. Mr. T. S. Eliot argues that Milton
introduces 'imagery which tends to distract us from
the real subject', but praises 'the happy introduction
of such extraneous matter', as in the simile of the
whale:

> Him haply slumbring on the *Norway* foam
> The pilot of some small night-founder'd Skiff,
> Deeming some Island, oft, as Sea-men tell,
> With fixed Anchor in his scaly rind
> Moors by his side under the Lee, while Night
> Invests the Sea, and wished Morn delayes:
> So stretcht out huge in length the Arch-fiend lay
> Chain'd on the burning Lake.

Eliot points out that we '*nearly* forget Satan in attending
to the story of the whale'; but he claims that as Milton
'recalls us just in time', the 'diversion strengthens, instead of weakening, the passage'. Leavis retorts that this
is inapt and misleading: 'Miltonic similes don't focus
one's perception of the relevant, or sharpen definition in
any way.' He will not tolerate what Eliot calls the 'inspired frivolity' of such passages, 'an enjoyment by the

author in the exercise of his own virtuosity, which is a mark of the first rank of genius.' But we have only to consider how much *Paradise Lost* would lose by the deletion of such passages to be glad that Milton allowed himself this freedom. For by means of the long epic simile he was able to bring within the compass of the poem, already concerned with the significant history of mankind from the Creation to the Last Judgement, a still wider range of experience—literary, mythological, geographical, cosmological. But the similes are nevertheless subordinated to the whole.

Whether or not we are recalled in time to the matter in hand depends very largely on the way the verse is read. Eliot is surely right in suggesting that the overcoming of the danger of our being lost in such digressive similes gives an additional pleasure. We may suspect that Leavis is so much taken up with his attempt to resist the verse-movement that he does not give Milton much of a chance. Why should the reader resist? However foreign the idiom, however uncolloquial the diction and the rhythm, however long and oratorical the verse-paragraphs, it can scarcely be doubted that Milton is successful in dictating to us by means of the rhythm, as surely if he had recorded it on a disc, how the verse is to be read. The emphasis falls unerringly on the words which should be stressed. Dr. Leavis seems to imply that the sound of the verse has no relation to the sense, and that the reader tries in vain to introduce sensitive intonations into the lines; but if we willingly surrender ourselves to the ritual, abandoning all attempt to transform Milton into a dramatic poet, we shall find that sense and rhythm are perfectly married. There is little justification for Eliot's complaint that we cannot attend to meaning and sound at the same time, though we may suspect that some of the critics who have spoken eloquently about the organ-music have not bothered too much about the sense. Milton can hardly be blamed for this.

We may take as an example part of Eve's first speech:

> Sweet is the breath of morn, her rising sweet,
> With charm of earliest Birds; pleasant the Sun
> When first on this delightful Land he spreads
> His orient Beams, on herb, tree, fruit, and floure,
> Glistring with dew; fragrant the fertil earth
> After soft showers; and sweet the coming on
> Of grateful Eevning milde, then silent Night
> With this her solemn Bird and this fair Moon,
> And these the Gemms of Heav'n, her starrie train:
> But neither breath of Morn when she ascends
> With charm of earliest Birds, nor rising Sun
> On this delightful land, nor herb, fruit, floure,
> Glistring with dew, nor fragrance after showers,
> Nor grateful Evening mild, nor silent Night
> With this her solemn Bird, nor walk by Moon,
> Or glittering Starr-light without thee is sweet.

It will be observed that Eve's list of seven pleasures is repeated in the second half of the speech with subtle variations, so that the recurrence gratifies the ear without wearying it with mere repetition. The purpose of the repetition is withheld until the last four words of the passage, with a firm emphasis on the *thee*, and a return in the last word, *sweet*, to the first word of the complete sentence. There is nothing peculiar in the diction. The epithets, though quietly suitable, are in no way startling. The effect is obtained not by brilliance of phrase, nor by striking imagery, but by the general movement of the whole passage. The language is not magniloquent, and certainly not un-English. Only twice does the poet allow himself a departure from the normal word-order; 'nor rising Sun / On this delightful land' (a phrase which is condensed from one in the earlier part of the speech) and

'grateful Evening mild' which exhibits the favourite Miltonic trick, derived from the Classics, of sandwiching a
noun between two epithets. Some readers may feel that
Eve has marshalled her clauses and her repetitions with
such rhetorical artifice that she gives the impression not
of conversing with her husband on their honeymoon in
Eden, but of delivering an oration to him. But the mother
of mankind may properly be given a more than regal dignity, even apart from the necessity Milton felt of observ-
ing the proprieties of the secondary epic. Milton, perhaps, used a style a good deal more remote from the
colloquial than Virgil did, and at times, though rarely, we
may be inclined to sympathize with Johnson's complaint
of 'Babylonish dialect' and with Keats's feeling that the
poem was 'a corruption of our Language'.[1]

We may turn now to wider questions of structure and
meaning. In accordance with the traditional epic structure, Milton 'hastes into the midst of things'. We are
first introduced to the rebel angels, after they have been
defeated and cast into hell, plotting to seduce Adam and
Eve. In the fourth book Satan arrives in Eden, and we
meet Adam and Eve for the first time. In the next four
books Raphael comes to warn Adam of his danger, and to
that end describes the war in heaven and the creation of
the world; Adam, in his turn, describes his first meeting
with Eve. These four books, therefore, are largely concerned with events which took place before those
described in the first four. In Books 9 and 10 Milton
recounts his central story, man's first disobedience, and
the repentance of Adam and Eve. In the last two books
Michael gives a prophetic account of the remote effects
of the Fall in the history of mankind, and in particular

---

[1] There is a useful defence of Milton's diction in Arnold Stein's *Answerable
Style* (1953), pp. 119–62. It has recently been suggested by F. T. Prince that
Milton's epic style was influenced by the practice of the Italian poets. See
The Italian Element in Milton's Verse (1954).

the redemption of man by Jesus. Half the poem, therefore, is concerned with events which take place before or after the central episode. Just as Æneas describes the fall of Troy to Dido, so Raphael describes the war in heaven to Adam; and just as Virgil at the end of the *Æneid* looks forward to the future history of Rome, so Milton gives us a miniature history of the world. In place of the great national epic we have the epic of the Fall and Redemption of Man.

Satan is not the real hero of the poem, as Dryden pretended, being misled by the theories of the epic current in his day; but many readers have felt that the first two books, in which Satan is the dominating figure, are poetically superior to the later books, and that Satan is a more effective poetical figure than either Adam or Christ. As Werblowsky points out, the imagery used by Milton in describing Satan and his followers is much more vivid than that used to describe the celestial angels who are treated with 'stepmotherly niggardliness'. But, human nature being what it is, all poets find it easier to depict evil than good, Milton's powers were declining by the time he wrote the concluding books, and, from the nature of the subject, the opening books are more exciting than those which describe events after the Fall. Above all, a poet has 'as much delight in depicting an Iago as an Imogen', and Milton as poet delighted in the exercise of his power.

Waldock, however, complained of the way in which Milton, realizing that Satan was becoming too sympathetic, inserted continual reminders of his wickedness.

> If one observes what is happening one sees that there is hardly a great speech of Satan's that Milton is not at pains to correct, to damp down and neutralize. He will put some glorious thing in Satan's mouth, then, anxious about the effect of it, will pull us gently by the sleeve, saying (for this

is what it amounts to): 'Do not be carried away by this fellow: he *sounds* splendid, but take my word for it . . .' We have in fact, once again, the two levels: the level of demonstration or exhibition, and the level of allegation or commentary; and again there is disagreement. What is conveyed on the one level is for a large part of the time not in accord with what is conveyed on the other.

We may take as an example of this 'technique of degradation' Milton's comment after Satan's first speech:

> So spake th' Apostate Angel, though in pain,
> Vaunting aloud, but rackt with deep despare.

Waldock asserts that the speech is really incompatible with despair, and that it is naïve to suppose that the comment is as valid as the speech. It seems to me, on the contrary, to be the kind of speech which might well come from one who was over-compensating for his own despair. There is no reason why we should take Satan's speeches at their face value, and little reason why Milton should not insert stage-directions in this way. The grandeur of the epic style, at its most magnificent in the first two books, might otherwise mislead us, as the quality of the poetry put into the mouth of Macbeth and Othello has led some critics to whitewash those two characters. Keats came up against a similar difficulty in writing *Hyperion*. In the first version he gave Saturn a great speech which was intended to be the expression of feebleness and despair. In *The Fall of Hyperion* Keats deliberately weakened the speech so that his commentary could be expressed by the feebleness of the words themselves. Keats has done more or less what Waldock thinks Milton should have done with Satan; but the result, though psychologically truer, is much weaker as poetry. Milton, in beginning his epic, naturally made Satan as sublime a figure as possible. He had to hold the attention of the reader; if there was to be a real conflict between good and evil, he had to provide God with an antagonist not wholly contemptible; and he had to give the devil his due. Those critics who complain that Milton's portrait of the rebel angels was too sympathetic seem to overlook two important points. It was not necessary for a seventeenth-century reader to put in a 'good morning's hate of Satan' as a protection against too much sympathy: he believed in Satan and both by conviction and training he would hate him heartily. This means that he would be less likely than a modern reader to be swept away by the sheer grandeur of the poetry, and though he would be prepared to admit that Satan possessed certain good qualities, he would tend to think that heroism when exerted in the worst of causes ceased to be a virtue. Gangsters are often brave, but it is only the immature who think that they should therefore be admired. The other point sometimes overlooked is that Milton is careful to point out that Satan's

> form had yet not lost
> All her Original brightness, nor appear'd
> Less then Arch Angel ruin'd, and th' excess
> Of Glory obscur'd.

We must assume that what is said of his appearance is true also of his character. He becomes more obviously evil in the course of the poem. Some critics maintain that the Satan of the later books *could* not have developed from the heroic figure of Book 1. But although Milton does not show us the stages by which Satan deteriorates, there should be no great difficulty in believing that damnation has such an effect.

It is true that Milton adopts a double standard. Belial is condemned by the standards of epic courage, and Satan, who is sufficiently heroic by those standards, is condemned by Christian standards. Yet Belial, though perhaps for the wrong reasons, proposes a policy of acquiescence in the Divine will which is not very different from the resignation required later of Adam; and, on the other hand, the good angels and Christ Himself in the war in heaven display the traditional epic heroism.

Several critics have complained of various kinds of inconsistency in the descriptions of Hell. It is odd, for example, that the devils are doomed to dwell 'In Adamantine Chains and penal Fire', and that Satan himself is chained on the burning lake, while a few lines later they are all able to fly to dry land, and before long they are engaged in all kinds of activities. Milton himself explains that all-ruling Heaven has allowed them freedom so that they may heap further damnation on themselves, an explanation that gives one a repulsive conception of the deity. Waldock is right to point out that in other hells 'the damned have come to the end of their road'; but in Milton's, though it is a place of punishment, the damned are full of plans for the future. Milton (says Waldock) was trying 'to accomplish two incompatible things', namely, to depict a hell which was a place of perpetual torment, and one which was a base for military operation. But is this necessarily a weakness? It is demanded by the fable that the devils should continue their struggle by other means; and as Hell had only just been founded and devils are different from human souls, we must not expect the same laws to operate. Waldock says that as the rebel angels are little inconvenienced by their situation, we cannot take the lurid descriptions of tortures very seriously, so that Hell 'loses most of its meaning'. But Milton makes clear that the tortures are intermittent, and there is no reason why we should not assume that they are not partly symbolic. The angels have been driven out from bliss, and that has always been the worst part of damnation. It may be, as Mr. Eliot suggests, that we should 'not attempt to *see* very clearly any scene that Milton depicts'; the world to which he has introduced us does not require this kind of consistency. 'It should be accepted as a shifting phantasmagory'. Leavis and Waldock both feel that Milton's Hell is not 'consistently realized'; but to some readers the very inconsistencies give a nightmare quality which could not have been achieved in any other way.

About the poetical quality of the great speeches in Book 2 all critics are agreed. They depend for their effect on a superb use of certain rhetorical devices, on the way they are logically constructed, if on false premises, and on the sustained power of the verse, but hardly at all on imagery. If one compares them with an oration in one of Shakespeare's plays, one notices a vast difference between them. Ulysses's speech to Achilles in *Troilus and Cressida*, for example, loses all its power if it is paraphrased and stripped of its imagery. The twenty-five images, each one evolving naturally from the one before, vividly present the effect of time on reputation; without the images the bare argument could be reduced to a sentence. But Milton's speeches would retain much of their force even in a paraphrase. The five spokesman are well distinguished: Moloch, who counsels open war since their situation cannot possibly be worse than it is; Belial who counsels 'ignoble ease, and peaceful sloath' because he realizes that they are certain to be defeated again; Mammon who thinks they can lead a tolerable existence in Hell; Beëlzebub who suggests that they capture the earth or seduce Man to their party; and Satan who volunteers to make the perilous journey. Quite properly Milton endows his devils with human characteristics, and it is difficult to see how the psychology of defeat could be more effectively displayed.

The first two books of *Paradise Lost* maintain such a high level of poetry that Milton set himself a well-nigh impossible task in the remainder of the poem. The third book begins magnificently with the invocation to Light—perhaps the high-water mark of Milton's poetry—and the first sight we have of God is not unworthy of it:

> About him all the Sanctities of Heaven
> Stood thick as Starrs, and from his sight receiv'd
> Beatitude past utterance; on his right
> The radiant image of his Glory sat,
> His onely Son . . .

But as soon as God starts to speak—like a school divine, as Pope puts it—we are conscious of a sudden deterioration in the quality of the poetry. Coleridge is one of the few critics who has made a whole-hearted defence of this part of the poem:

> Pope was hardly the man to criticise Milton. The truth is, the judgment of Milton in the conduct of the celestial part of his story is very exquisite. Wherever God is represented as directly acting as Creator, without any exhibition of his own essence, Milton adopts the simplest and sternest language of the Scriptures. He ventures upon no poetic diction, no amplification, no pathos, no affection. It is truly the Voice of the Word of the Lord coming to, and acting on, the subject Chaos. But, as some personal interest was demanded for the purposes of poetry, Milton takes advantage of the dramatic representation of God's address to the Son, the Filial Alterity, and in those addresses slips in, as it were by stealth, language of affection, or thought, or sentiment.

This defence may seem plausible until we turn to the poem itself. The story of the Fall, perhaps inevitably, shows God in an unamiable light, and Milton does not improve matters by allowing Him to indulge in the kind of self-justification that is apt to sound like excuses. It is true that His foreknowledge of the Fall did not pre-determine it, but Waldock is right in saying that the speech in which God blames Adam and Eve in advance gives us a clear 'impression of nervousness, insecurity and doubt':

> They themselves decreed
> Thir own revolt, not I: if I foreknew,
> Foreknowledge had no influence on their fault,
> Which had no less prov'd certain unforeknown.
> So without least impulse or shadow of Fate,
> Or aught by me immutablie foreseen,
> They trespass, Authors to themselves in all
> Both what they judge and what they choose; for so
> I formed them free, and free they must remain,
> Till they enthrall themselves; I else must change
> Thir nature, and revoke the high Decree
> Unchangeable, Eternal, which ordain'd
> Thir freedom, they themselves ordain'd thir fall.

If this apologia had been put into the mouth of one of the angels, or if it had formed part of the poet's own commentary, it would have been less offensive, for we could then assume that God had a better case than its exponents had been able to put. But when God Himself indulges in theological argument we are tempted to point out the flaws. Waldock thinks that 'it does not come very naturally to Milton to suggest a loving God'. This is not true of the young Milton, and though it may apply to the disillusioned Milton of 1660, I doubt whether this is the cause of his failure in Book 3. The real trouble is due partly to the nature of the subject, partly to the weaknesses of Puritan theology (from which Milton was not wholly emancipated, and to which we are no longer sympathetic), and partly to the difficulty of writing about the three persons of the Trinity. If the Son is portrayed as merciful, the Father, if only for dramatic reasons, is likely to seem stern and legalistic. First 'God Almighty comes with a Thump on the Head', said Blake, 'and Jesus Christ comes with a balm to heal it.'

Milton recovers himself at the point when God asks if anyone will die for Man:

> And silence was in Heav'n: on mans behalf
> Patron or Intercessor none appeerd,
> Much less that durst upon his own head draw
> The deadly forfeiture, and ransom set . . .

This passage, the speech in which Christ offers Himself for the redemption of man, and the hymn sung by the Heavenly Choir (372–415) show that Milton's failure was only temporary. The whole of the next book maintains and even surpasses this level. It begins with Satan's great soliloquy which culminates in his reversal of values: 'Evil be thou my Good.' Although Dr. Leavis has complained of the sensuous poverty and the generalized description of Eden, I think Mr. C. S. Lewis's defence of the passage is both brilliant and true. Milton creates for us the sensation of paradise, not by direct description, which would be inappropriate, but by careful preparation and suggestion. He does not want to give us 'his own private image of the happy garden,' as Eliot, for example, does in *Four Quartets*. 'While seeming to describe his own imagination he must actually arouse ours.' He does this by allowing us to approach Eden with Satan, so that we feel its remoteness and inaccessibility; and our expectations are aroused as we ascend higher and higher, as though a camera were moving gradually up the tall trees and over the verdurous wall of paradise. The air becomes purer, we catch strange perfumes on the breeze, and at last we arrive. The description which follows contains all the obvious ingredients—golden fruit, roses without thorns,

Groves whose rich Trees wept odorous Gumms and
    Balme—

but, as Mr. Lewis says, 'the unexpected has here no
place.' Milton clinches his effect by comparing Eden
with other earthly paradises:

> Not that faire field
> Of *Enna*, where *Proserpin* gathring flours
> Her self a fairer Floure by gloomie *Dis*
> Was gatherd, which cost *Ceres* all that pain
> To seek her through the world; nor that sweet Grove
> Of *Daphne* by *Orontes*, and th'inspir'd
> *Castalian* Spring might with this Paradise
> Of *Eden* strive; nor that *Nyseian* Ile
> Girt with the River *Triton*, where old *Cham*,
> Whom Gentiles *Ammon* call and *Libyan Jove*,
> Hid *Amalthea* and her Florid Son
> Young *Bacchus* from his Stepdame *Rhea's* eye;
> Nor where *Abassin* Kings thir issue Guard,
> Mount *Amara*, though this by som suppos'd
> True Paradise under the *Ethiop* line
> By *Nilus* head, enclos'd with shining Rock,
> A whole dayes journey high, but wide remote
> From this *Assyrian* Garden, where the Fiend
> Saw undelighted all delight . . .

The grove sacred to Apollo near Antioch, and the neighbouring Castalian spring, the island of Nysa off the coast
of Libya, where the infant Bacchus and his mother were
hidden, and the hill of Amara where, according to
Heylin, there were thirty-four palaces in which the
younger sons of the Emperor were shut up, were all
secluded, beautiful and deceptively secure—like Eden.
The Castalian spring is contrasted with the Heavenly
Muse; the false paradise of Amara, a prison in disguise,
is contrasted with the true paradise of Eden; and the
hiding of Bacchus is perhaps an analogue of the flight into

L

Egypt, and certainly recalls the story of Semele who, like Eve, wanted too much divinity and was punished for her presumption. The fate of Prosperine also finds a parallel in the fate of Eve: she too is 'gathered' by the ruler of the underworld, and the parallel is underlined by Milton just before he describes the Fall.

The account of the war in Heaven is not altogether satisfying. Johnson argued that it was necessary for Milton to invest his angels with form and matter, but that he should have kept 'immateriality out of sight'. Mr. Lewis, on the other hand, thinks that Milton actually believed in the kind of angels he depicted. But he does not succeed in making *us* believe in them. He starts off well by making Raphael explain to Adam that his account of the war must not be taken literally:

> What surmounts the reach
> Of human sense, I shall delineate so,
> By lik'ning spiritual to corporal forms,
> As may express them best, though what if Earth
> Be but the shadow of Heav'n, and things therein
> Each to other like, more then on earth is thought?

Yet when we come to the battle we are sometimes compelled to take the action symbolically, and sometimes literally. There are some details which remind us of Homeric battles (the wearing of armour, for example), others (such as when the combatants hurl hills at each other) which remind us of mythological wars, and others again (such as the use of gunpowder) which are anachronistic by any standard. There is undeniably a good deal of inconsistency; and it is impossible for us to suspend our disbelief when Milton is continually slipping from one convention into another. Only in the last phase of the battle (824–865) when the Son goes into action in his chariot of wrath, paralysing all resistance, does Milton silence all objections. This passage displays an extra-ordinary energy and power, and it is undoubtedly one of the great moments of the poem.

Book 7 opens with an invocation of Urania, the Heavenly Muse; and Milton takes the opportunity, at this half-way house, of referring to his position at the Restoration. Most of the book is taken up with Raphael's account of the Creation, which is a good example of Milton's middle manner: there are no lapses, but equally no outstanding passages. In Book 8 Adam enquires about celestial motions, and Milton, in spite of his admiration for Galileo, is compelled to sit on the fence. This is not because he is clinging to revelation where it conflicts with the new science, but because he was compelled by the scheme of the poem to adhere to the ptolemaic theory, because the controversy between it and the Copernician theory was still going on, and it would have been unwise to come down on one side or the other, and because the controversy had no relevance to man's salvation. This is Raphael's point.

After Adam has described his first meeting with Eve, there is a crucial passage in which he confesses that his love for her is 'commotion strange'. He tells Raphael that, although he realizes that she is created his inferior,

> Yet when I approach
> Her loveliness, so absolute she seems
> And in her self compleat, so well to know
> Her own, that what she wills to do or say,
> Seems wisest, vertuousest, discreetest, best;
> All higher knowledge in her presence falls
> Degraded, Wisdom in discourse with her
> Looses discount'nanc't, and like folly showes;
> Authoritie and Reason on her waite,
> As one intended first, not after made
> Occasionally; and to consummate all,

Greatness of mind and nobleness thir seat
Build in her loveliest, and create an awe
About her, as a guard Angelic plac't.

Raphael scolds Adam for this confession, warns him not
to be led astray by outside appearances, urges him to set
a proper value on himself, tells him that he shares his
sexual instinct with the animals, and enjoins him to use
earthly love as a scale by which to ascend to heavenly
love. Adam protests that he loves Eve for her manners
and character rather than for her external beauty or from
sexual desire, and that his reason is not subjected. Adam
has received a good deal of sympathy from modern
critics: they complain that Raphael's homily is un-
pleasant and dishonest, since he deliberately ignores
Adam's qualifying remarks. Waldock suggests that
Adam 'has already had his thoughts refined and his heart
enlarged'. But the point is surely that Raphael recog-
nizes that Adam is in danger of allowing his reason to be
swayed by his love—as indeed it turns out—and Raphael's
'contracted brow' is due to his realization that it is only
a step from saying that 'All higher knowledge in her
presence falls Degraded' to an abdication from responsibility. He is, perhaps, more swayed by passion than he
realizes or is prepared to admit. In the moral scheme of
the poem, where freedom is inseparable from right
reason, Adam has not yet fallen; but Raphael wisely
warns him of the danger.

Although Mr. Eliot is right in saying that Adam and
Eve are prototypes, rather than types, and that 'were they
more particularized they would be false', we should
notice that in the remaining books of the poem Milton
allows himself a considerable degree of psychological
realism. He prepares the way for the actual Fall with
admirable artistry. Eve's dream, related at the beginning
of Book 5, in which she eats the forbidden fruit and flies

up to heaven, prepares her mind, as it does ours, for her
actual fall. Of course, as Adam tells her,

> Evil into the mind of God or Man
> May come and go, so unapprov'd, and leave
> No spot or blame behind.

There is no reason to agree here with Dr. Tillyard, who
argues that as the dream has disturbed Eve so much, she
cannot be entirely innocent. But the dream is a fore-
runner of the temptation to which she later succumbs.
Adam, as we have seen, is in danger of allowing his emotions to govern his reason; but the real beginning of the
Fall does not come until the ninth book, when Eve suggests that they should each work on their own so that
they can get more work done. Adam tells Eve that he is
afraid Satan may seize the opportunity if they separate
even for a while. Eve replies, a trifle hurt, but 'with
sweet austeer composure' that she never expected to
hear he doubted her ability to resist temptation. Adam
then tries to excuse himself by saying a temptation is an
aspersion on the tempted, even if it is unsuccessful,
and that he himself receives 'access in every Vertue'
from the influence of Eve's looks. Eve replies reasonably
that they would gain double honour by rejecting temptation, and plausibly that she cannot praise a fugitive and
cloistered virtue. Adam tells her that they should not
seek temptation, since 'Trial will come unsought' and
since

> Reason not impossibly may meet
> Some specious object by the Foe subornd,
> And fall into deception unaware.

He urges her to 'approve First thy obedience'. Then,
foolishly, he gives way at the very moment when Eve is
prepared to obey him. His excuse is that now they have
been warned they will be more vigilant alone than they

would be together. Having obtained the permission she wants, Eve professes to have been convinced by this last fallacious argument:

> From her Husbands hand her hand
> Soft she withdrew.

She departs on her fatal journey to temptation:

> O much deceav'd, much failing, hapless *Eve*,
> Of thy presum'd return! event perverse!
> Thou never from that houre in Paradise
> Foundst either sweet repast, or sound repose;
> Such ambush hid among sweet Flours and Shades
> Waited with hellish rancor imminent
> To intercept thy way, or send thee back
> Despoild of Innocence, of Faith, of Bliss.

Already in this dialogue Eve has displayed the pride, however venial, and Adam the weakness, however amiable, which afterwards lead to their downfall. It is here, rather than later, that Adam is 'fondly overcome with Femal charm'.

The temptation itself is a magnificent achievement. Satan appeals first to Eve's pride, and then to her curiosity. He flatters her beauty, and tells her she ought to be a Goddess with plenty of admirers. Eve does not at once repudiate the 'friendly' flattery: she is curious to know how the serpent had become endowed with speech. This gives Satan his opportunity. He describes the effects of a particular fruit—without mentioning it comes from the forbidden tree—and he adds some more flattery of Eve as the 'Sovran of Creatures'. Eve now repudiates the flattery, but asks to be shown the tree. When he leads her to the forbidden tree, she immediately declares that to eat of it is the one thing she may not do. Eve is still innocent, and Satan up to this point has merely been weakening her resistance: he now begins the temp-

tation in earnest. He shows that she will not die from
eating the fruit since it gives 'Life to Knowledge'; that
God has not punished the serpent for eating, and that it
would be absurd to forbid men what is allowed to beasts;
that God has threatened death merely to test her courage;
that God would be unjust if He punished them for 'such
a petty Trespass'; that if He is unjust, He cannot be God
and should not be obeyed; and that God is jealous and
doesn't want men to become godlike.

It is all very plausible. The speech, says Waldock,

> is crammed with specious argument, with sequences that
> look like syllogisms but stop before they have arrived, with
> stretches of reasoning that sound as if they are reaching a
> conclusion but do not quite reach it; and the ground is
> shifted every few seconds. What seems the same argument
> has turned in the twinkling of an eye into one that is really
> its opposite.

Furthermore, though Eve was not to know this, the
reasoning is all based on a lie: the serpent is not a real
serpent who has acquired the gift of speech through eating of the Tree of Knowledge. Eve, to protect herself,
had either to be very quick at spotting logical fallacies—
and Milton assumed that women were less good at reasoning than men—or else she had to fall back on the prohibition, and assume that the serpent must be evil
because he was advising her to disobey God's command.
As soon as she starts to listen to argument she is lost.
She even provides an additional argument: that God
Himself has named the Tree of Knowledge, and apparently forbidden them to be wise.

Although the fruit seems to have aphrodisiac properties, the act of eating it would have been harmless if it
had not been forbidden. This, as Mr. Lewis points out,
was St. Augustine's view. It was also Milton's, clearly
stated in *Christian Doctrine*. If modern readers are inclined

to agree with Satan that the eating of the apple was a petty trespass, Milton has this answer:

> If the circumstances of this crime are duly considered, it will be acknowledged to have been a most heinous offence, and a transgression of the whole law. For what sin can be named, which was not included in this one act? It comprehended at once distrust in the divine veracity, and a proportionate credulity in the assurances of Satan; unbelief; ingratitude; disobedience; gluttony; in the man excessive uxoriousness, in the woman a want of proper regard for her husband, in both an insensibility to the welfare of their offspring, and that offspring the whole human race; parricide, theft, invasion of the rights of others, sacrilege, deceit, presumption in aspiring to divine attributes, fraud in the means employed to attain the object, pride and arrogance.

Here, one cannot help feeling, Milton is protesting too much. Almost any sin, even the most venial, could by special pleading be made to sound as monstrous. Milton seems to be engaged in a struggle to convince himself that the Fall was as bad as it is painted. In the poem, as Waldock points out, he is something of an opportunist. The prime fact of the Fall was disobedience (as we can see from the very first line of the poem); but the causes of Eve's disobedience cannot be covered by a simple formula. There is no reason why they should be; but this is why different critics have seized upon different explanations—pride, levity, injured merit, passion usurping the place of reason. Adam also is guilty of disobedience, but the causes of his disobedience are quite different from those of Eve's. He has been weak, giving way to Eve's plan of separation; but his actual fall is due partly to what has been called gregariousness or the social bond, and partly to what some call uxoriousness and others call love. Love is the more appropriate word.

Eve after eating the fruit decides first she will make herself Adam's superior; and then remembering that the fruit may be deadly she decides at the thought of Adam wedded to her successor that he shall share with her in bliss or woe. Adam, meanwhile, is waiting with a garland of flowers for her return. When he hears what Eve has done, he immediately decides to share her fate:

> How art thou lost, how on a sudden lost,
> Defac't, deflour, and now to Death devote? . . .
> Certain my resolution is to Die;
> How can I live without thee, how forgoe
> Thy sweet Converse and Love so dearly joyn'd,
> To live again in these wilde Woods forlorn?
> Should God create another *Eve*, and I
> Another Rib afford, yet loss of thee
> Would never from my heart; no no, I feel
> The Link of Nature draw me: Flesh of Flesh,
> Bone of my Bone thou art, and from thy State
> Mine never shall be parted, bliss or woe.

This soliloquy of the unfallen Adam contrasts with the soliloquy of the fallen Eve just before. Both, for very different reasons, found it intolerable to contemplate a second Eve. Although theoretically we must condemn Adam's disobedience, since his duty to God is higher than his love, few readers will wish, in their heart of hearts, that he had acted otherwise. Milton, perhaps because he had identified himself too much with Adam, arouses our sympathies so much that we are tempted to feel that the God who had imposed the arbitrary ban ought to be delighted that Adam, animated by a pure and self-sacrificing love, had dared to disobey. But this, of course, is to read the poem with modern eyes. We have to accept the theological assumptions of the poem, and Milton is quite right to pull himself up sharply and remind us that Adam, by putting his love for Eve above his duty to God, has been overcome by female charm. This does not mean that Adam sinned because Eve exercised on him the arts of female persuasion, and still less that he was carried away by sensuality. It means merely that he set his love for his wife above his duty to God. Dean Inge has said that the Devil always tempts an Englishman in the guise of his wife and family.

Waldock complains with some justice that when God comes to judge the sinful pair Adam is his own worst advocate. 'His testimony is unfair to himself and to Eve and amounts to a nearly total misrepresentation of what really occurred.' But we are no doubt meant to assume that Adam's false account is 'one of the earliest results of the Fall itself', and I cannot see that Waldock is justified in his later complaint that Adam's account becomes the official view of the poem. When the Son asks:

> Was shee thy God, that her thou didst obey
> Before his voice, or was shee made thy guide?

He is not necessarily accepting Adam's account as true. He is showing that even if it were true his conduct would be inexcusable.

We must pass over the moving reconciliation of Adam and Eve in Book 10 and the brilliantly grotesque account of Satan's return to Hell. The last two books are poetically on a much lower level, but they are essential to the scheme of the poem. Michael's outline of history is too brief for any episode to be very effective in itself, except the account of the Flood. Nevertheless, the last two hundred lines of the poem are of vital importance to our understanding of the whole. On being told of the redemption of man, Adam exclaims:

> O goodness infinite, goodness immense!
> That all this good of evil shall produce,
> And evil turn to good; more wonderful

> Than that by which creation first brought forth
> Light out of darkness! full of doubt I stand,
> Whether I should repent me now of sin
> By mee done and occasiond, or rejoyce
> Much more, that much more good thereof shall
>   spring,
> To God more glory, more good will to Men
> From God, and over wrauth grace shall abound.

Michael proceeds to tell Adam of the persecution of true Christians:

> heavie persecution shall arise
> On all who in the worship persevere
> Of Spirit and Truth; the rest, farr greater part,
> Will deem in outward Rites and specious formes
> Religion satisfi'd; Truth shall retire
> Bestuck with slandrous darts, and works of Faith
> Rarely be found: so shall the World goe on,
> To good malignant, to bad men benigne,
> Under her own waight groaning, till the day
> Appeer of respiration to the just
> And vengeance to the wicked . . .

There is a great contrast between this conception of the Second Coming and the one Milton had expressed before the Civil War. But the final moral is by no means pessimistic, though it may seem that Milton has turned his back on the Renaissance and his own great programme for the acquisition and advancement of learning. Michael tells Adam that the sum of wisdom is to acknowledge his redeemer:

> hope no higher, though all the Starrs
> Thou knewst by name, and all th'ethereal Powers,
> All secrets of the deep, all Natures works,
> Or works of God in Heav'n, Air, Earth, or Sea,
> And all the riches of this World enjoydst,
> And all the rule, one Empire; onely add

Deeds to thy knowledge answerable, add Faith,
Add Vertue, Patience, Temperance, add Love,
By name to come call'd Charitie, the soul
Of all the rest: then wilt thou not be loath
To leave this Paradise, but shalt possess
A Paradise within thee, happier farr.

Dr. Tillyard has suggested that the 'incomparable passion and force' with which Milton has here stated the doctrine of Christian humility are

> vastly increased when it is seen that the true crisis of *Paradise Lost* was a dramatic representation of that very doctrine, rendered all the weightier through the irony of the actors not realising what high principle their deeds were in fact setting forth.

The penitence of Adam and Eve, their reconciliation, and their courageous acceptance of their fate, illustrate the 'better fortitude of patience' and the Christian virtues mentioned by Michael. The moral is expressed plainly and prosaically. But we need not suppose that there Milton the theologian had taken the pen from the hands of Milton the poet. From the purely artistic point of view a bare statement of doctrine was necessary at this point. Adam and Eve can depart from Eden with the consolation that God has used their sin for his own purposes; that the way is open for them and their descendants to possess a paradise within them happier far than the one from which they are being expelled; that after the Second Coming the whole earth will be a happier place than Eden; and that their sin—*felix culpa*—has turned out for the best:

> They looking back, all th'Eastern side beheld
> Of Paradise, so late thir happie seat,
> Wav'd over by that flaming Brand, the Gate
> With dreadful Faces throng'd and fierie Armes:

Som natural tears they drop'd, but wip'd them soon;
The World was all before them, where to choose
Thir place of rest, and Providence thir guide:
They hand in hand with wandring steps and slow,
Through *Eden* took thir solitarie way.

The end of the poem is also a beginning.

It must be admitted, perhaps, that Milton does not fully succeed in justifying the ways of God to men, though he would have been more nearly successful to the readers of his own age. It must be admitted, too, that at moments Milton's poetic sympathies did not altogether coincide with his overt beliefs. It must be admitted that the scenes in Heaven are not so successful as the scenes in Hell and in Eden, and that some of the writing, especially in the last two books, falls below the level of the best. But when these admissions have been made, I doubt whether they are as damaging as some critics pretend. Although Dante was a greater poet than Milton, we do not judge the success of the *Divine Comedy* by its power to convince us of its truth. The rift between humanism and puritanism, between poetry and theology, between human sympathy and religious belief may set up stresses and strains in the structure of the poem: but it is impossible to wish that Milton had been more of a Puritan, because in that case he would have been more didactic and less poetical, and the characters of Satan, Adam and Eve would have been treated with less imaginative sympathy; and if he had been less of a Puritan he would not have been drawn to this particular subject. It may be that the greatness of the poem depends in a very real way on the tension between the two sides of Milton's mind and temperament.

In some great poems we feel that the shaping hand of the poet has extended to every image and every line, so that the total meaning is nothing more and nothing less

than the sum of the parts. Considered from this standpoint *Paradise Lost* is a partial failure. But its imperfections and contradictions are, to put the matter at its
lowest, of absorbing interest. As Mr. Werblowsky has
said, Milton embodies 'the dichotomy of European
consciousness equally deriving from Palestine and from
Greece'. Writing when he did, Milton could have
avoided this dichotomy completely only by being false
to one side of his nature. He expressed the conflict of
his age, and his poetry is great partly because it em-
braced so much. *Paradise Lost*, Waldock complained,
'cannot take the strain at the centre' because Milton's
theory of the Fall conflicts with his human sympathies.
This may be so; but perhaps the intolerable strain is itself
a proof of the poet's integrity.

There is some difference of opinion about the degree
of unorthodoxy in the theology of *Paradise Lost*. Professor Sewell argued that the poem, 'at least in the first
three or four books', represented 'an earlier state of
opinion than *De Doctrina Christiana*.' Professor Kelley,
on the other hand, believes that the two works agree in
theological dogma, and that they represent two different
treatments of a basic body of belief. This view is, I
believe, substantially correct, and it is therefore legitimate to use the treatise to throw light on the interpretation of the poem. But Mr. C. S. Lewis is also right in his
contention that Milton does not in the poem obtrude his
heresies. He wished his epic to be acceptable to
Protestants of all sects, so he used language which could
be interpreted in an orthodox way did we not have other
evidence of Milton's actual opinions. Mr. Lewis even
says that 'except for a few isolated passages' the doctrine
of the poem 'is not even specifically Protestant or Puritan. It gives the great central tradition' of Christianity.
Although numerous heresies have been attributed to

Milton, notably by Saurat, perhaps the only one of any real importance to the reader of *Paradise Lost* is his view of God the Son. There is no doubt that in his later years Milton was an Arian, denying the consubstantiality of Christ, and this affected both *Paradise Lost* and *Paradise Regain'd* to some degree. It is possible that some of the difficulties in which he became involved in his portrayal of events in heaven were partly due to his anti-Trinitarian views.

Although the theology of *Christian Doctrine* is deduced mainly from the Scriptures, it is important to remember that Milton recognized that the text of the Bible has come down to us through unreliable channels. 'It is difficult to conjecture', he says,

> the purpose of Providence in committing the writings of the New Testament to such uncertain and variable guardianship, unless it were to teach us by this very circumstance that the Spirit which is given to us is a more certain guide than Scripture, whom therefore it is our duty to follow.

In this, as Professor Willey has suggested, Milton 'is seen to be one of the rationalising theologians of the century'. He would not have agreed with Dryden that the light of reason was dim. He would rather have said with John Smith, 'To follow Reason is to follow God.'

Chapter Nine

PARADISE REGAINED

IN spite of Ellwood's story, *Paradise Regain'd* is not really a sequel to *Paradise Lost*, and we must assume that Milton was being ironical at the expense of the worthy but imperceptive Quaker. For already in the earlier poem he had shown how paradise could be regained— how man could overcome the effects of the Fall and possess an inner paradise far happier than the Eden he had lost. Yet the general reader is apt to regard *Paradise Regain'd* as a sequel, and to be conscious of the several ways in which it is inferior to its predecessor. Only too obviously it lacks the exciting story, the epic grandeur, the superb descriptions of *Paradise Lost*. It is singularly lacking in poetic ornament; it has very little imagery; there are few 'poetic' passages; and the style seems to be desiccated and prosaic, the work—the general reader is tempted to say—of a tired and exhausted poet, an ineffective attempt to emulate a past success. Worst of all, the sublime figure of Satan, arousing admiration even in his evil, has deteriorated into a Machiavellian politician: and Christ is no longer a martial hero but an able disputant, somewhat narrow in his views, and somewhat self-righteous into the bargain.

To compare the two poems is bound to result in feelings of disappointment, and it must be admitted that *Paradise Regain'd* will never arouse the unalloyed admiration of the general reader. Yet it has been admired, and by the people whose judgement must be respected,

Milton's fellow poets. Coleridge and Wordsworth both
thought it was the most perfect in execution of all Milton's poems, and other poets have concurred in this
verdict. It has been suggested that the difference between
such professional admiration and the opinion of the
general reader is largely because the poets appreciate the
difficulties of Milton's task, and pay tribute to the tech-
nical genius that overcame them. But it may rather be
due to the failure of the general reader to recognize the
class of poem to which *Paradise Regain'd* belongs, and to
the mistaken belief that Milton had tried and failed to
repeat his previous success. In some ways the poem is
nearer in genre to Dryden's *Religio Laici* than it is to
Paradise Lost. The argument is more important than the
action, and the verse is 'fitter for discourse and nearer
prose.' Yet Milton hardly ever lapsed, as Wordsworth
too often did, into the prosaic. The verse is sometimes
perilously deflated, but always by some inherent rhythmical tact Milton saves himself. Some critics have seen
in the poem the 'feebleness of senility'; and even in
Milton's own lifetime it was thought to provide evidence
for the decay of his genius. But if it displays less imaginative power than *Paradise Lost*, this was largely because the
subject would not allow it; and Milton was right to
claim that his poetic power was undiminished. Without
making any concessions to his readers, without deigning
to be obviously 'poetic', without providing any of the
extraneous pleasures which enable many readers to
imagine they are enjoying poetry, Milton created a work
of art more perfect, though not of course greater, than
his masterpiece. Its appreciation demands a more austere
taste than any other of Milton's poems; but its sublimities
are none the less real for escaping so narrowly the aridities
of middle age, the deserts of theological and political
controversy, and the harshness of disappointed idealism.

M

In *The Reason of Church Government* Milton had mentioned the possibility of writing a brief epic on the model of the book of *Job*; and having successfully accomplished the larger task of the 'diffuse' epic, he now sought to fulfil what had originally been an alternative ambition. *Paradise Regain'd* is not—any more than *Job*—strictly an epic poem. It is a philosophical dialogue on the problem of ends and means. It expands the Gospel story of the Temptation into 2,000 lines; but in spite of this expansion Milton cursorily dismisses the first and third temptations in fifty lines, concentrating on the second.

Theologians had often discussed the significance of the three temptations and it was generally agreed that they symbolized what St. John called the lust of the flesh, the lust of the eyes and the pride of life; and these were equated with the flesh, the world and the devil, and also with the three temptations in one, to which Adam and Eve had succumbed. Sometimes, however, the king-doms-of-the-world temptation was associated with the devil. Milton, following the Protestant view, did not believe that the first temptation was one of greed; he makes it clear that it was rather 'distrust in God'. He introduced the banquet scene, not as a repetition of the temptation of bread, but as one of greed. In his treatment of the third temptation—cast thyself down—Milton departed from tradition. The devil does not really tempt Jesus. He wishes to find out (as he has done in accordance with tradition throughout the poem) whether Jesus is the Son of God. He sets Jesus on the pinnacle of the temple expecting Him to fall, and supposing that He will either be killed or else saved by angelic intervention. In either case, Satan will discover what he wants to know. But Jesus answers ambiguously:

It is written
Tempt not the Lord thy God.

This is often taken to mean: 'It is wrong for me to test God's miraculous powers;' but a more probable meaning is 'Do not test me, the Lord your God.' Jesus announces His identity and proves it by not falling. As Professor Elizabeth Marie Pope has argued,

> to bring the theme to a full and perfect conclusion within the poem, Satan obviously ought to be made aware of the Lord's true identity at the last, though not in the manner which he had foreseen, or which gratified him in the least.

But Milton was strongly impelled by tradition to deal directly with the temptations of the flesh, the world and the devil; and he did this by comprising them all under Satan's temptation.

We may also suspect that although the three temptations were all applied by theologians to the basic temptations to which ordinary men were liable, Milton was mainly interested in the second. The temptation to turn stones into bread or to cast himself down from the temple were ones to which he could be prone only in some symbolic or allegorical way. Milton, moreover, seems to have been singularly indifferent to the supernatural powers with which Jesus is credited. He was concerned almost entirely with Jesus as the divine exemplar, a pattern to which every man could aspire. It was the second temptation alone which was literally relevant to Milton's own problems: Satan offered to Jesus all the kingdoms of the world if he would fall down and worship him. In discussing this temptation, Milton is answering the perennial question, whether it is legitimate to use unworthy means for the achievement of noble ends, whether, indeed, it is possible to achieve noble ends by ignoble means—whether the Kingdom of God can be founded on earth by the use of force.

It is clear that the discussion of these questions gave

Milton a further opportunity of holding an inquest on the
failure of the English Revolution. The debate between
Satan and Jesus is not a mere academic argument, un-
exciting because the victory of Jesus was preordained,
and irrelevant to humanity at large because the dis-
putants were supernatural: it is an engrossing dialogue on
political ethics, made poignant by Milton's own experience. Once again he is justifying God's ways to
Englishmen, making Jesus his mouthpiece. This does not
mean, as some critics have suggested, that Milton's hero
was a self-portrait. In fact he was at pains to draw a
credible picture of the historical Jesus, depicting Him
with the limitations, as well as the virtues, of a Jew living
in the early days of the Roman Empire. When Satan
shows Athens to Jesus, he retorts that all Greek philosophy is inferior to that of the Old Testament prophets:

> As men divinely taught, and better teaching
> The solid rules of Civil Government
> In thir majestic unaffected stile
> Than all the Oratory of *Greece* and *Rome*.
> In them is plainest taught, and easiest learnt,
> What makes a Nation happy, and keeps it so,
> What ruins Kingdoms, and lays Cities flat.

And as for the arts:

> If I would delight my private hours
> With Music or with Poem, where so soon
> As in our native Language can I find
> That solace?

We cannot assume that Milton himself in his old age had
grown so unlike himself as puritanically to dismiss the
Greek literature he had loved from his youth, of which
indeed the influence is apparent both in *Samson Agonistes*
and in *Paradise Regain'd* itself. Mr. Frank Kermode has
pointed out[1] that like St. Augustine Milton is contrast-

[1] *The Review of English Studies*, 1953, p. 328.

ing 'the dissension of the gentile philosophers in favour
of the concord of the canonical scriptures'. But he does
not make such sacrifices easily, and 'there is in this section of the poem a profound and moving turbulence.'
But although Milton may here have been writing in
character, it must be admitted that in one or two
passages, as when Jesus characterizes the mob—

> Of whom to be disprais'd were no small praise—

Milton does seem to obtrude his own bitterness.

The relevance of the second temptation to the poet's
political disillusionment was the main reason why he
chose to write the poem. He wished once more to
explain the failure of his hopes of seeing the Kingdom
established in his lifetime; and he shows that freedom
depends on self-discipline. Jesus declares that God's
kingdom will not come by political action, but only by
the guiding of

> Nations in the way of truth
> By saving Doctrine.

If Milton, despairing of politics, now hoped to spread
true Christianity by means of the *De Doctrina*, as critics
have plausibly suggested, he had parted with one illusion
only to embrace another: for, in the first place, it was
extremely unlikely that he would ever find a publisher for
so heretical a treatise; secondly, those most competent
to understand its significance would have been the read-
iest to reject it as heresy; and, thirdly, even if the ideas
expressed in it had gained universal currency, they
would have had little effect on human behaviour. It is
doubtful, indeed, whether a man who subscribed to
Milton's heresies would be distinguishable in his actual
behaviour from any other protestant.

Yet it would unfairly limit the meaning of *Paradise*

Regain'd to relate it too closely to Milton's own programme. The main argument, that the Kingdom could
not be established by Satan's means, has a universal significance; and most readers would agree that persuasion
and conversion, rather than force and miracle, are the
only means that can fruitfully be employed. It is not surprising that Wordsworth and Coleridge, who had enter-
tained high hopes on the outbreak of the French Revolution and had been woefully disillusioned, should have
admired the poem in which Milton expressed his wiser
and more balanced disillusionment, even as their own
poetic revolution enabled them to recognize the magnificent austerity of Milton's poem. We have had plenty
of opportunities during the last twenty years of reading
the testaments of those who have become disillusioned
with politics, and they are likely to give us a high opinion
of Milton's refusal to rest in disillusionment or to bow
the knee to Baal.

In *Paradise Lost* Milton had turned his back on the heroism depicted in pagan epics to sing 'the better fortitude
of Patience and Heroic Martyrdom'. In *Paradise Regain'd*
even more obviously, he was showing the superiority of
the Christian hero—in this case Christ Himself—to the
heroes of the past. As Mr. Kermode has shown, Christ
is not merely exemplary in his character and conduct,
but he gains 'exemplary rewards, which transcend the
rewards of pagan heroism'. The temptation of the banquet 'is essential to the structure of the poem' because it
shows Jesus rejecting 'the banquet of sense, so that he
may attain to the higher angelic banquet'; and he rejects
earthly glory for 'that which is measured by the knowledge of God'. He shows himself as the exemplary hero
by 'confuting or transcending all the known modes of
heroism'.

The general reader may admit the interest of the poem

for the light it throws on Milton's later opinions, for its penetrating treatment of the problem of ends and means, and even for its portrait of the Christian hero, and yet complain that considered strictly as poetry it is not a success. But it is easy to show by quotation that Milton still possessed the evocative power he had displayed in *Paradise Lost*, as for example in the description of the banquet:

> all Fish from Sea or Shore,
> Freshet, or purling Brook, of shell or fin,
> And exquisitest name, for which was drain'd
> *Pontus*, and *Lucrine* Bay, and *Afric* Coast.
> Alas how simple, to these Cates compar'd,
> Was that crude Apple that diverted *Eve*!
> And at a stately side-board, by the wine
> That fragrant smell diffus'd, in order stood
> Tall stripling youths rich-clad, of fairer hew
> Than *Ganymed* or *Hylas*, distant more
> Under the Trees now trip'd, now solemn stood
> Nymphs of *Diana's* train, and *Naiades*
> With fruits and flowers from *Amalthea's* horn,
> And Ladies of th' *Hesperides*, that seem'd
> Fairer than feign'd of old, or fabl'd since
> Of Fairy Damsels met in Forest wide
> By Knights of *Logres*, or of *Lyones*,
> *Lancelot* or *Pelleas*, or *Pellenore*.

Here is the old power—the stately music, the sonorous names, the evocative allusions—and no one reading this passage would notice any falling away from the poetic level of *Paradise Lost*. How exquisite, too, is the direct allusion to the central episode of the earlier poem, and the felicity of the word 'diverted'! But such passages are rare in *Paradise Regain'd*, and Milton generally writes in a more austere style. As an illustration, we may take an earlier passage from the Second Book:

It was the hour of night, when thus the Son
Commun'd in silent walk, then laid him down
Under the hospitable covert nigh
Of Trees thick interwoven; there he slept,
And dream'd, as appetite is wont to dream,
Of meats and drinks, Natures refreshment sweet;
Him thought, he by the Brook of Cherith stood,
And saw the Ravens with their horny beaks
Food to *Elijah* bringing Even and Morn,
Though ravenous, taught to abstain from what they
    brought:
He saw the Prophet also how he fled
Into the Desert, and how there he slept
Under a Juniper; then how awakt,
He found his Supper on the coals prepar'd,
And by the Angel was bid rise and eat,
And eat the second time after repose,
The strength whereof suffic'd him forty days;
Sometimes that with Elijah he partook
Or as a guest with *Daniel* at his pulse.
Thus wore out night, and now the Herald Lark
Left his ground-nest, high towring to descry
The Morn's approach, and greet her with his Song:
As lightly from his grassy Couch up rose
Our Saviour, and found all was but a dream,
Fasting he went to sleep, and fasting wak'd.

Here there is no obvious beauty, no decoration, no
imagery. The effect is obtained by subtle rhythmical
variations, by an occasional rhetorical departure from the
prose order of words, by the pun on 'ravenous', by an
apt choice of Biblical allusion, and by a simple but exquisite diction—the kind of simplicity which is never
found in the early work of poets, and which seems to
result from a process of purification. It is a style that
(like the best of Wordsworth's) continually risks the
charge of being prosaic; but it saves itself by what one
can only call spiritual integrity. The style of *Paradise*

Regain'd is a triumph of character. It is also a triumph of the art which comes with long experience of writing.

Until recently it was assumed that *Samson Agonistes* was written after *Paradise Regain'd*, and in spite of Professor W. R. Parker's attempt to show that it was written much earlier, between 1646 and 1653, there is enough internal evidence to suggest that it was written after the Restoration, either when Milton was in hiding, or else, and more probably, not long before its publication. For although we may reject emphatically any idea that *Samson Agonistes* is an allegory of the poet's own life— blind among enemies though he was—this does not mean that the poem was merely a Biblical tragedy with no relevance to Milton's own time. Just as Shakespeare deliberately introduced references to the Gunpowder Plot into *Macbeth*, in such a way that his audience must have been conscious of the deliberate anachronism, so Milton, we are driven to believe, introduced references to the state of the nation after 1660. Even if we accepted the earlier date of composition, we should have to assume that Milton revised the poem fifteen or twenty years later.[1]

---

[1] Cf. W. R. Parker, *Philological Quarterly* (1949), pp. 145 ff. He points out that Milton's nephew makes no mention of the writing of *Samson Agonistes*, as he does of *Paradise Regain'd*; that the presence of rhyme suggests an earlier date than that of *Paradise Lost*; that the irregular lines of the Latin ode to John Rouse may be compared with the irregular form of the choruses; that critics are prejudiced in favour of the traditional date by their tendency to regard the poet as the hero of the poem, though Milton himself attacks the practice of interpreting poetry as veiled autobiography in his *First Defence*, where he says that words are put into the mouths of characters, 'as is most fitting to each character, not such as the poet would speak if he were speaking in his own person.' Nevertheless, there is no doubt that Milton did sometimes speak through his characters, and there are references in *Samson* which would be difficult to relate to the years when Professor Parker thinks it was written. One negative piece of evidence may be mentioned. In his verses on *Paradise Lost* Marvell has the couplet:

> So Sampson groap'd the Temples Posts in spight,
> The world o'rewhelming to revenge his sight.

It is surely unlikely that Marvell would have written these lines in a poem in praise of his friend if *Samson* were already in existence.

Milton, however egotistical, was never merely personal in his poetry. 'His true self', as Sir Herbert Grierson has said, 'is his ideals, the good old cause, and the English people.' There are, it is true, passages in the play which seem to be based on Milton's personal experience, as when he refers to the sufferings of the righteous—

> perhaps in poverty
> With sickness and disease thou bow'st them down,
> Painful diseases and deform'd,
> In crude old age—

or to the blindness of the hero. But nothing could better demonstrate Milton's greatness as an artist than a comparison of the five uses to which he put his experience of blindness. The two private sonnets, the invocation to Light in Book 3 of *Paradise Lost*, a passage in the *Second Defence*, and the opening speech of Samson are all appropriate to the kind of thing Milton was writing at the moment—personal, epic, or dramatic—and there is no reason why he should not have utilized the original shock at the loss of his eyes, though it had been experienced fifteen years before. On the other hand, there are passages which seem designed to point a contemporary moral and to remind the reader of the immediate relevance of the theme. When, for example, the chorus laments that God forsakes the righteous, Milton must have been thinking of the fate of the regicides and the unjust execution of Vane:

> Oft leav'st them to the hostile sword
> Of Heathen and prophane, thir carkasses
> To dogs and fowls a prey, or else captiv'd:
> Or to the unjust tribunals, under change of times,
> And condemnation of the ingrateful multitude.

In his picture of the Philistines Milton seems to have

taken the victorious Royalists as his model. After the Restoration, from the point of view of the Puritans, God had been blasphemed :

> God,
> Besides whom is no God, compar'd with idols,
> Disglorified, blasphem'd, and had in scorn
> By th'Idolatrous rout amidst thir wine.

The position of Samson resembles that of the defeated Puritans. He is held up to obloquy as a 'Murtherer, a Revolter, and a Robber'; he is condemned to captivity 'Among inhuman foes'; he is deserted by most of his friends;

> Blind, disheartn'd, sham'd, dishonour'd, quell'd,

he can see no way of serving his country:

> To what can I be useful, wherein serve
> My Nation, and the work from Heav'n impos'd,
> But to sit idle on the household hearth,
> A burdenous drone.

A modern critic, Mr. Pettet, has complained that Milton was too egotistical in his religious poetry, and that *Samson Agonistes* deals with a comparatively superficial religious problem—God's apparent desertion of his faithful champions. Certainly this is one of the themes of the play; but Milton seldom dealt directly or personally with his religious problems. Instead of writing of the conflict in his own heart between the Humanist and the Puritan, he embodied it in the story of *Comus*. Instead of writing of his own disillusionment with his fellow-countrymen, he wrote of the Fall of Man; instead of writing of the failure of the English Revolution, he wrote of the problem of ends and means as embodied in the story of the Temptation; and in *Samson Agonistes* he utilized the Biblical story for the expression of his doubts and the recovery of his faith. That the sense of desertion expressed in the play may have been experienced by the poet some years before meant merely that the emotion was recollected in tranquillity.

Dr. Johnson complained about the construction of the play that it had a beginning and an end, but no middle. He did not realize that the action takes place mainly in the mind of the hero. At the beginning of the play we find him weighed down by despair and longing for death:

> So much I feel my genial spirits droop,
> My hopes all flat, nature within me seems
> In all her functions weary of herself;
> My race of glory run and race of shame,
> And I shall shortly be with them that rest.

Nothing is left to him but

> Faintings, swounings of despair
> And sense of Heav'ns desertion.

He is the more depressed because he had felt himself to be chosen by God for such tasks, 'high exploits, Full of divine instinct'. He had once been the nursling and choice delight of heaven. He had grown up under God's 'special eye' and now, through his own fault, his high hopes have been brought to nothing. Both Samson and the chorus reiterate that God is not to blame:

> Nothing of all these evils hath befall'n me
> But justly. I myself have brought them on,
> Sole Author I, sole cause.

The ways of God are just, the Chorus declare, 'and justifiable to men'. In such speeches Milton is referring not to his personal misfortunes but to the failure of the English people; but when the chorus complain that God seems to desert his chosen, Milton may be thinking of himself.

> But such as thou hast solemnly elected
> With gifts and graces eminently adorn'd
> To some great work, thy glory,
> And people's safety, which in part they effect:
> Yet toward these thus dignifi'd, thou oft
> Amidst thir highth of noon,
> Changest thy countenance, and thy hand with no
>   regard
> Of highest favours past
> From thee on them, or them to thee of service.

At the end of the play the Chorus are brought to a final realization that

> All is best, though we oft doubt,
> What th'unsearchable dispose
> Of highest wisdom brings about,
> And ever best found in the close.
> Oft he seems to hide his face,
> But unexpectedly returns.

The theme of the play is this recovery of faith after disillusionment and doubt—a theme which can hardly be regarded as 'comparatively superficial'.

In the enslaved and blinded Samson Milton was depicting, as more than one critic has suggested, the England of the Restoration, enslaved to monarchy, and spiritually blind. The English people might have set up an ideal commonwealth which would have prevented the return of the monarchy and, through the mouth of Samson, Milton upbraids his countrymen for re-enslaving themselves:

> But what more oft in Nations grown corrupt,
> And by thir vices brought to servitude,
> Then to love Bondage more than Liberty,
> Bondage with ease then strenuous liberty;
> And to despise, or envy, or suspect
> Whom God hath of his special favour rais'd

> As thir Deliverer; if he aught begin,
> How frequent to desert him, and at last
> To heap ingratitude on worthiest deeds?

Samson in Dalila's 'lascivious lap' may represent England after 1660; and at times Dalila herself seems to speak for the England which had betrayed the good old cause. She pleads her weakness and is told by Samson that

> All wickedness is weakness: that plea therefore
> With God or Man will gain thee no remission.

She tells him that she was urged by the priests and magistrates that it was her duty to entrap a common enemy; and Samson replies:

> if aught against my life
> Thy countrey sought of thee, it sought unjustly,
> Against the law of nature, law of nations,
> No more thy countrey, but an impious crew
> Of men conspiring to uphold thir state
> By worse than hostile deeds, violating the ends
> For which our countrey is a name so dear;
> Not therefore to be obey'd.

But mingled with Milton's attacks on England for consenting to the counter-revolution, there is the hope that God would intervene to overthrow the enemy:

> all the contest is now
> 'Twixt God and *Dagon* . . .
> *Dagon* must stoop, and shall e're long receive
> Such a discomfit, as shall quite despoil him
> Of all those boasted Trophies won on me,
> And with confession blank his worshippers.

The story of Samson was one which had always had a special significance for the poet. At the end of the *Reason of Church Government* there is the long passage in which he compares Charles I to Samson, the bishops to Dalila, and the laws to Samson's locks. A few years

later, when he wrote *Areopagitica* he compared England
to an eagle and to a Samson-figure, 'rousing herself like a
strong man after sleep, and shaking her invincible locks'.
So in the great chorus after the triumph of Samson he is
compared first to an eagle, and then to a phoenix, symbol
of resurrection.

> So vertue, giv'n for lost,
> Deprest, and overthrown, as seem'd,
> Like that self-begott'n bird
> In the *Arabian* woods embost,
> That no second knows nor third,
> And lay e're while a Holocaust,
> From out her ashie womb now teem'd
> Revives, reflourishes, then vigorous most
> When most unactive deem'd,
> And though her body die, her fame survives,
> A secular bird, ages of lives.

There is, therefore, nothing inherently improbable in
the theory that the hero of *Samson Agonistes* is, amongst
other things, a symbol of England.[1] Perhaps, as has been
suggested, Milton in this chorus was prophesying the
resurrection of the cause to which he had devoted most
of his life.

Yet it would be wrong to over-emphasize the political
significance of the poem. Professor F. Michael Krouse
has shown in *Milton, Samson and the Christian Tradition* that
Samson was a much more significant figure in the seventeenth century than he is now. He was regarded as a
saint and in certain respects a symbol of Christ—the
birth of both was foretold by an angel, both willingly
went to their deaths and both were betrayed with a kiss

[1] Mr. Wilson Knight has brought together in an interesting chapter in his
Chariot of Wrath the Samson references in Milton's earlier writings, and
thereby supported the theory that Samson can in some measure be identified
with England. He has a detailed comparison of the *Areopagitica* passage and the
Phoenix chorus.

—and he was thought to be the originai of Hercules. The significance of the epithet *Agonistes* is that Samson underwent a spiritual rather than a physical struggle: he was fighting the good fight.

> In the very title of this tragedy Milton invited his readers to think of Samson as a model of virtue, as a hero, as a champion of God, as a saint, a martyr, and a counterpart of Christ.

All Milton's chief works are concerned with temptations—*Comus*, *Paradise Lost*, *Paradise Regain'd*—and *Samson Agonistes* is no exception. The triple temptation of the flesh, the world, and the devil is repeated in a different form. Manoa offers his son liberty and peace, and since he seems to have no more chance of following his vocation as God's champion, this represents the temptation by necessity, the temptation of the flesh. Dalila, though she is, of course, a seductress, uses the arts of fraudulent persuasion. This is the temptation of the world. Harapha represents the temptation of the Devil. As in *Paradise Regain'd* he tempts by violence and fear. Samson rejects the three temptations and so regains his strength and dies gloriously. Christ had overcome the wiles of Satan in *Paradise Regain'd* and served as an exemplar for man. Samson, though in one sense a prototype of Christ, also demonstrated how an ordinary man could similarly overcome temptation and so regain Paradise.

Mr. J. Middleton Murry's horror that Milton should end his career as a poet with the spiritual and poetic self-sufficiency of *Samson Agonistes* and with a bloodthirsty, if imaginary, revenge on his adversaries, was apparently caused mainly by his assumption that the poet merely dramatized the primitive story from the *Book of Judges*. If Professor Krouse is right to suggest that Milton was influenced, though not circumscribed, by the traditional interpretations of the story in the seventeenth century, we can see that the play was Christian as well as Hebraic, and that it is a remarkable blend of Greek form with Christian content. It is possible, too, as Mr. Frank Kermode recently suggested, that Milton was attempting to imitate some of the characteristics of Hebrew poetry. Yet Shakespeare, the great secular poet of the English Renaissance, ended his work with a plea for forgiveness and mercy; the great poet of the Puritan Reformation offers us only 'calm of mind, all passion spent.' To us there is no doubt as to which attitude is the more Christian; but to most of Milton's contemporaries, who had been waging a holy war for thirty years, there would have seemed to be nothing unchristian in Milton's recalcitrance. They would have admitted with him that there were times when God demands a 'dolorous blast' of the trumpet.

The style of *Samson Agonistes* has been variously judged. Dr. Leavis regards it as intolerably insensitive, and 'at its shocking worst' in the rhymed choruses. He adds sarcastically:

> One can grant that it might possibly help to form taste; it certainly could not instil or foster a love of poetry. How many cultivated adults could honestly swear that they had ever read it through with enjoyment?

This question seems to me to be a kind of intellectual blackmail, for if we admit that we know adults who have read *Samson Agonistes* more than once and with undiminished pleasure, Dr. Leavis can always retort that, according to the exacting standards of *Scrutiny*, our friends and acquaintances are 'uncultivated'. To some critics, however, the blank verse exhibits a noble austerity, the more impressive because it was not the result of initial poverty or of failing powers. Even the superficial

N

naïvety of the rhyming of the final chorus, which appears to one critic to resemble in its syntax the attempt of a scholar, whose knowledge of the classics is greater than that of his mother tongue, to translate a chorus from a Greek play, may to others appear as suitable in its context as the quotations from religious writers on which Eliot relies at certain moments in *Four Quartets*. Anything more sensuous or displaying a more lively sensibility would be more shocking than Milton's flat statements in which he weds the Aristotelian theory of tragedy to religious sentiment:

> His servants he with new acquist
> Of true experience from this great event
> With peace and consolation hath dismist
> And calm of mind all passion spent.

This is the only chorus written entirely in rhymed verse, and it has the effect, after the occasional rhymes and assonances of the earlier choruses, of rounding off the whole play. The re-affirmation of faith finds its metrical equivalent in the rhymes for which the chorus had seemed earlier to be fumbling.

In view of Dr. Leavis's objections to the choruses of the play, it may be worth while to quote the praise of a poet who can hardly be accused of academic prejudice. In a letter to Dixon, Gerard Manley Hopkins declared:

Milton's art is incomparable, not only in English literature but, I should think, almost in any; equal, if not more than equal, to the finest of Greek or Roman. And considering that this is shown especially in his verse, his rhythm and metrical system, it is amazing that so great a writer as Newman should have fallen into the blunder of comparing the first chorus of the *Agonistes* with the opening of *Thalaba*. . . . Milton having been not only ahead of his own time as well as all after-times in verse-structure, but these particular choruses being his own high-water mark.

In spite of his admiration for Shakespeare's plays Milton had at one time thought of writing a tragedy in the classical form on the subject of Macbeth. In the preface to *Samson Agonistes* he defended tragedy as 'the gravest, moralest, and most profitable of all other Poems' and vindicated it from 'the small esteem, or rather infamy, which in the account of many it undergoes at this day.' As he thought that Aeschylus, Sophocles and Euripides were 'unequall'd yet by any, and the best rule to all who endeavour to write Tragedy', Milton wrote his play on the classical model. It was never intended for the stage, but it is the one English classical tragedy that can be regarded as more than an interesting experiment, and it has been performed with some success. It was a fitting swansong for the most classical of English poets.

Chapter Ten

CONCLUSION

MILTON's later poems and the second edition of the minor poems were published in an age which was antipathetic to his poetic as well as to his political ideals. It was an age when Denham and Waller were regarded as the reformers of our numbers, the age of Dryden's early poems and heroic plays, the age of Etherege and Wycherley. But although the veteran Waller dismissed *Paradise Lost* as long and tedious, it was appreciated by Denham, Dryden and others who had no sympathy with Milton's political views. Even in the poet's lifetime he had found the fit audience, though few, for whom he had avowedly written, and in the space of twenty-one years the epic sold at least 2,500 copies.

With the Glorious Revolution of 1688 Milton's prose acquired some popularity, and it is noteworthy that in the farcical scene at the end of *The Beaux' Stratagem* Farquhar echoed *The Doctrine and Discipline of Divorce*. Addison expounded the beauties of *Paradise Lost* for the middle-class readers of *The Spectator* and it was Milton's example that led many eighteenth-century poets to use blank-verse for their longer poems—from *The Seasons*, *The Grave* and *Night Thoughts* to *The Pleasures of the Imagination*, *The Task*, and *The Excursion*. Milton's influence is equally apparent in the poetic diction of the period—though this derives also from Dryden and Pope. Yet the reaction against the poetic diction at the end of the century did not prevent Wordsworth, Shelley, Keats,

Byron, Blake and Coleridge from being considerably influenced by Milton's poetry.

Although many minor poets in the eighteenth and nineteenth centuries wrote badly under Milton's influence, and although his blank verse was not a suitable medium for an account of the woollen industry or of the manufacture of cider, it may be doubted whether his influence on the greater poets was as detrimental as some critics have thought. Wordsworth's blank verse and his use of the sonnet form, though owing something to Milton's example, are unmistakably his own; the opening of *The Fall of Hyperion* is sufficient proof that Keats had freed himself from undue subservience to *Paradise Lost*; and Blake's *Milton* displays a great poet correcting the damnable errors of his greater predecessor. Hopkins, who developed his characteristic rhythms partly by studying Miltonic prosody, admired and did otherwise, as a great poet should. In the twentieth century, the better poets could learn more from the Jacobean dramatists, Donne and Marvell, Baudelaire, Valéry and Rilke, more even from Whitman and Laforgue, than they could from Milton. The last long poems of consummate excellence were Wordsworth's *Prelude* and Byron's *Don Juan*: it is fairly clear that all epic poems of the foreseeable future will be abortive—or in prose. But *Paradise Lost* remains, with all its manifest imperfections, the most magnificent undramatic poem in the language. It is the one English poem which can without absurdity be put in the same class as the *Iliad*, the *Æneid* and the *Divine Comedy*, even though it falls below them within that class. It is as superior to the *Lusiad* and *Jerusalem Delivered* as it is to *The Prelude* and *Don Juan*.

Even apart from *Paradise Lost*, Milton's other masterpieces would be enough to ensure his place amongst the greatest English poets. The exquisite felicity of the best of the shorter poems in the 1645 volume, the almost un-flawed loveliness of *Comus* and *Lycidas*, and the austere grandeur of *Paradise Regain'd* and *Samson Agonistes* keep a central place in English poetry. Animating them all is the lofty spirit of a great man. Of course he was violent in controversy, somewhat humourless, egotistical, not one to suffer fools gladly, and sometimes unforgiving. But on the evidence of his early biographers, who are a safer guide than legal documents to an understanding of his character, he was also warm-hearted and generous, and one who never lacked the affection of numerous friends. If he was unduly proud, he pilloried his pride in the portrait of Satan; he made sacrifice after sacrifice for the causes in which he believed; and his steadfastness and courage in adversity exemplified the 'better fortitude of Patience'.

SELECT BIBLIOGRAPHY

A. *Original Editions*

A MASKE (1634).

OBSEQUIES TO THE MEMORY OF MR. EDWARD KING (1638), containing LYCIDAS.

EPITAPHIUM DAMONIS (1640).

OF REFORMATION TOUCHING CHURCH-DISCIPLINE IN ENGLAND (1641).

OF PRELATICAL EPISCOPACY (1641).

ANIMADVERSIONS UPON THE REMONSTRANT'S DEFENCE AGAINST SMECTYMNUS (1641).

THE REASON OF CHURCH-GOVERNMENT URG'D AGAINST PRELATY (1641-2).

AN APOLOGY AGAINST A PAMPHLET CALL'D A MODEST CONFUTATION OF THE ANIMADVERSIONS UPON THE REMONSTRANT AGAINST SMECTYMNUS (1642).

THE DOCTRINE AND DISCIPLINE OF DIVORCE (1643).

OF EDUCATION (1644).

THE JUDGEMENT OF MARTIN BUCER, CONCERNING DIVORCE (1644).

AREOPAGITICA (1644).

TETRACHORDON (1645).

COLASTERION (1645).

POEMS (1645).

THE TENURE OF KINGS AND MAGISTRATES (1649).

OBSERVATIONS UPON THE ARTICLES OF PEACE (1649).

EIKONOKLASTES (1649).

JOANNIS MILTONI ANGLI PRO POPULO ANGLICANO DEFENSIO (1650).

A LETTER WRITTEN TO A GENTLEMAN IN THE COUNTRY (1653).

DEFENSIO SECUNDUS (1654).

DEFENSIO PRO SE (1655).

A TREATISE OF CIVIL POWER IN ECCLESIASTICAL CAUSES (1659).

CONSIDERATIONS TOUCHING THE LIKELIEST MEANS TO REMOVE
HIRELINGS OUT OF THE CHURCH (1659).

BRIEF NOTES UPON A LATE SERMON (1660).

THE READIE AND EASIE WAY TO ESTABLISH A FREE COMMON-
WEALTH (1660).

PARADISE LOST (1667).

THE HISTORY OF BRITAIN (1670).

PARADISE REGAIN'D . . . SAMSON AGONISTES (1671).

POEMS (1673).

OF TRUE RELIGION, HAERESI, SCHISM, TOLERATION (1673).

EPISTOLARUM FAMILIARUM . . . PROLUSIONES (1674).

MR. JOHN MILTON'S CHARACTER OF THE LONG PARLIAMENT
(1681).

A BRIEF HISTORY OF MOSCOVIA (1682).

LETTERS OF STATE . . . TOGETHER WITH SEVERAL OF HIS POEMS
(1694).

OF CHRISTIAN DOCTRINE, translated from the Latin by C. R.
Sumner (1825).

B. *Modern Editions*

The initials—e.g. (C)—are those used for reference in
the text. Editions with * are particularly recommended.

THE COLUMBIA UNIVERSITY EDITION of Milton's Works, under
the general editorship of F. A. Patterson, 20 vols. (1931–
1941). (The only complete edition.) (C)

*THE STUDENTS' MILTON, by F. A. Patterson (1930; revised
1933). (All the verse and most of the prose, with annota-
tions.)

*COMPLETE POETRY AND SELECTED PROSE, by E. H. Visiak
(1938). (The attractive Nonesuch edition.)

PROSE WORKS, by J. A. St. John, 5 vols. (1848–53). (The Bohn
edition, the text of which is not altogether reliable, is
relatively inexpensive.)

THE YALE UNIVERSITY EDITION OF MILTON'S PROSE, by D. A.
Wolfe (1954–).

*MILTON'S PROSE, by M. W. Wallace (1925) (cheap selection).

*THE POETICAL WORKS OF JOHN MILTON, by H. C. Beeching (1900; revised 1938).

THE POEMS OF JOHN MILTON, by H. J. C. Grierson, 2 vols. (1925).

Annotated editions include the following:

*THE CAMBRIDGE MILTON FOR SCHOOLS, by A. W. Verity, 10 vols. (1891–6).

MR. JOHN MILTON'S POEMS, by C. Brooks and J. E. Hardy (1951). (A reprint of the 1645 volume with valuable critical commentaries.)

*MINOR POEMS, by B. A. Wright (1938).

SONNETS, by J. S. Smart (1921).

FACSIMILE OF THE MANUSCRIPT OF MILTON'S MINOR POEMS, by W. A. Wright (1899).

PARADISE REGAINED, by L. C. Martin (1925).

LATIN POEMS, by W. MacKellar (1930). (M)

PRIVATE CORRESPONDENCE AND ACADEMIC EXERCISES, by P. B. and E. M. W. Tillyard (1932). (T)

PARADISE LOST, by H. Darbishire (1953). (Textually important.)

C. *Biographical*

THE LIFE OF MILTON, by D. Masson, 7 vols. (1858–81).

MILTON, by M. Pattison (1879).

EARLY LIVES OF MILTON, by H. Darbishire (1932).

MILTON, by R. Macaulay (1934).

MILTON ON HIMSELF, by J. S. Diekhoff (1939).

MILTON'S CONTEMPORARY REPUTATION, by W. R. Parker (1940).

THE LIFE RECORDS OF JOHN MILTON, by J. M. French (1949).

JOHN MILTON, ENGLISHMAN, by J. H. Hanford (1950). (H)

D. *Critical*

THE SPECTATOR, by J. Addison, 18 essays (1712).

LIVES OF THE ENGLISH POETS, by S. Johnson (1779).

THE MARRIAGE OF HEAVEN AND HELL, by W. Blake (1790).

MILTON, by W. Blake (1805).

S. T. Coleridge. Remarks on Milton are scattered through his lectures, his table-talk, his notebooks, and his letters.

J. Keats. There are comments on Milton in the LETTERS and there are some marginalia on PARADISE LOST.

MIXED ESSAYS, by M. Arnold (1879).

ESSAYS IN CRITICISM, by M. Arnold (Second series, 1888).

MILTON'S PROSODY, by R. Bridges (1893; revised 1901).

MILTON, by W. Raleigh (1900).

MILTON: MAN AND THINKER, by D. Saurat (1925).

A MILTON HANDBOOK, by J. H. Hanford (1926, 1946).

MILTON, by E. M. W. Tillyard (1930).

REVALUATION, by F. R. Leavis (1936).

A NOTE ON THE VERSE OF JOHN MILTON, by T. S. Eliot (1936).

MILTON, by T. S. Eliot (1947).

(Both these essays are reprinted, with cuts, in *Selected Prose*, 1953.)

MILTON AND WORDSWORTH, by H. J. C. Grierson (1937).

MILTON'S DEBT TO GREEK TRAGEDY IN 'SAMSON AGONISTES', by W. R. Parker (1937).

THE MILTONIC SETTING, by E. M. W. Tillyard (1938).

HEAVEN—AND EARTH, by J. M. Murry (1938).

THIS GREAT ARGUMENT, by M. Kelley (1941). (The best study of Milton's theological views.)

MILTON IN THE PURITAN REVOLUTION, by D. M. Wolfe (1941).

A PREFACE TO 'PARADISE LOST', by C. S. Lewis (1942).

MILTON AND THE PURITAN DILEMMA, by A. Barker (1942).

CHARIOT OF WRATH, by G. W. Knight (1942).

ENGLISH LITERATURE IN THE EARLIER SEVENTEENTH CENTURY, by D. Bush (1945).

PARADISE LOST IN OUR TIME—SOME COMMENTS, by D. Bush (1945).

FROM VIRGIL TO MILTON, by M. Bowra (1945).

MILTON'S 'PARADISE LOST', A COMMENTARY ON THE ARGU-MENT, by J. S. Diekhoff (1946).

PARADISE LOST AND THE SEVENTEENTH-CENTURY READER, by B. Rajan (1947).

PARADISE LOST AND ITS CRITICS, by A. J. A. Waldock (1947).

PARADISE REGAINED: THE TRADITION AND THE POEM, by E. M. Pope (1947).

MILTON'S SAMSON AND THE CHRISTIAN TRADITION, by F. M. Krouse (1949).

MILTON CRITICISM, by J. Thorpe (1951).

STUDIES IN MILTON, by E. M. W. Tillyard (1951).

THE COMMON PURSUIT, by F. R. Leavis (1952).

LUCIFER AND PROMETHEUS, by R. J. Z. Werblowsky (1952).

ANSWERABLE STYLE, by A. Stein (1953).

THE ITALIAN ELEMENT IN MILTON'S VERSE, by F. T. Prince (1954).

HEROIC KNOWLEDGE, by Arnold Stein (1957).

IMAGES AND THEMES IN FIVE POEMS BY JOHN MILTON, by Rosemond Tuve (1957).

SOME GRAVER SUBJECT, by J. B. Broadbent (1960).

A CRITIQUE OF 'PARADISE LOST', by John Peter (1960).

Note

Recent editions of Milton's works include the second volume of H. Darbishire's edition of the poems (1955); B. A. Wright's edition (1956); *Samson Agonistes*, edited by F. T. Prince (1957); *Milton's Dramatic Poems*, edited by G. and M. Bullough (1958).

INDEX